Standards for College and University Learning Resources Programs: Technology in Instruction

Second Edition

Association for Educational Communications and Technology
1126 Sixteenth Street, N.W., Washington, D.C. 20036

This publication can be purchased from the ASSOCIATION FOR
    EDUCATIONAL COMMUNICATIONS AND
    TECHNOLOGY
    1126 Sixteenth Street, NW, Washington, DC 20036

Formerly published under the title of:
    STANDARDS FOR COLLEGE AND UNIVERSITY
    LEARNING RESOURCES PROGRAMS, AECT Task
    Force II, Association for Educational Communications and
    Technology, Copyright 1982 by AECT. All rights reserved.

Library of Congress Cataloging-in-Publication Data

Standards for college and university learning
    resources programs.

        Authors: Richard A. Cornell and others.
        Bibliography: p.
        1. Media programs (Education)--Standards--United States.
2. Universities and colleges--United States--Departments--Standards. I.
Cornell, Richard A., 1933. II. Association for Educational
Communications and Technology.
LB1028.4.S72 1989 378'.17'078   86-70684
ISBN 0-89240-045-5

Copyright © 1989 by the Association for Educational Communications and Technology. All Rights reserved except those which may be granted by Sections 107 and 108 of the Copyright Revision Act of 1976.

Printed in the United States of America.

TABLE OF CONTENTS

Preface iv
Forward v
    Introduction vii
    Learning Resources Program vii
    Definition vii
    Purpose viii
    Scope viii
    Benefits viii

PART I: THE STANDARDS
Institutional Standards 1
Management Standards 2
    Director of LRP 2
        Knowledge 2
        Attitude 3
        Skill 3
    LRP Information Structure 3
        Goals, Objectives 3
        Plans 4
        Organization 4
        Policies, Procedures 4
        Communication 4
        Evaluation 5
    LRP Financial Structure 5
        Budget 5
        Current Value 6
Program Standards 6
    Design & Development Function 6
        Instructional Design 6
        Faculty Development 7
    Creative/Production Function 7
        Visualization Service 8
        Audio Service 8
        Combined Creative Services 8

Distribution Function 8
    Equipment Distribution 8
    Electronic Distribution 9
    Microcomputer Accessability 9
    Media/Resources 10
    Microcomputer Software 10
Maintenance and Engineering Function 11

PART II: SELF-STUDY RESOURCES
Introduction to Self-Study Resources 13
LRP Self-Study Checklist & Quantitative Guidelines 14
    Institutional Checklist 14
    Management Checklist 15
    Program Standards Checklist 21
LRP Self-Study Narrative 32
Management/LRP Director Evaluation Techniques 33
Management/LRP Director Essay Evaluation Instrument . 34
User LRP Evaluation Techniques 36
    User LRP Evaluation 36
    Suggested User Evaluation Items 36
Towards a Model LRP 38

APPENDIX A: Sample USER LRP Questionnaire 39
APPENDIX B: Equipment Depreciation Schedule 53
APPENDIX C: References 57
APPENDIX D: Contributors 61

PREFACE

Educators in colleges and universities nationwide have been waiting for a document such as this and its predecessor, *Standards for College and University Learning Resources Programs* (AECT 1982) for over 20 years. The late Jim Finn urged that we prepare a work regarding the development of standards for learning resources programs in the 1950s. Some 10 years later William Fulton headed a group whose aims were similar to those addressed by this document. In 1965 Gene Faris and Mendel Sherman headed an NDEA Title V research project whose objectives were also directed toward the accomplishment of the same goals.

In 1971 Galen Kelly chaired AECT's Task Force IV. Although no definitive standards emerged, that group published significant findings that emerged as an AECT publication in 1977: *College Learning Resource Programs: A Book of Readings*. In 1977 AECT also published another related work: Irving R. Merrill and Harold A. Drob's *Criteria for Planning the College and University Learning Resources Center*.

These standards are a significant reaffirmation of the work done by these pioneers. The work required to produce the present document was that of hundreds of professionals over many years, and not just that of those whose names appear within it.

Members of AECT's Postsecondary Guidelines: Task Force II began work on the current document in 1979, We rewrote it numerous times and had it reviewed by 25 selected postsecondary institutions. We scrutinized over 34 sets of standards published by constituent members of the Council on Postsecondary Accreditation (COPA).

An important decision, made in 1981, was to delete the term "guidelines" from the title in favor of "standards." Both the members of the Task Force and those who attended open hearings on the project felt that the word "standards" carried a more proactive connotation and sense of urgency. In 1982, *Standards for College and University Learning Resources Programs* was published, primarily through the efforts of Paul Marsh, the late Marian Hinz, and Robert Hinz.

The present document reflects many improvements over the first edition. A section has been added, for example, that specifically addresses the use of microcomputers in instruction. In order to improve the flow and continuity, several elements from the first edition have been rearranged into a more logical sequence. Finally, several sections have been added that should make the standards easier to implement. These latter changes can be credited primarily to Robert Spears, who was invited by the University of Houston to actually apply the standards to their own self-study efforts.

Both this work and the 1982 edition could not have been accomplished without the benefit of many others. A portion of our recognition clearly belongs to our predecessors, and it is gladly given. We would also like to thank those members of the Council on Postsecondary Education who so generously provided the committee with copies of their own standards. We also acknowledge the contributions of both past and present members of Task Force II - now known as the Postsecondary Guidelines Committee. Each of them, as well as our numerous volunteers, worked long and hard to make this edition a reality.

Finally, we would like to dedicate this edition to Marian Hinz, a charter member of the Task Force and a key contributing member of the Guidelines Revision Team. In May 1985, Marian passed away after a sudden illness. Right up to our final writing meeting earlier in 1985, Marian was an integral and valued member of our group. Her passing has left within each of us a void that cannot be filled.

This document then is for you, the director of learning resources, or you, the director of instructional technology services, or whatever title it is that identifies what you do. It is also for you, the college or university provost, chancellor, or president. More likely than not you, the vice-president for academic affairs, will be the one charged with implementing these standards.

View this work not as the ultimate solution for which you've been searching, but just for what it claims to be: a set of standards. These standards, like the profession in which we work, will be constantly changing to meet the needs of those whom each of us serves.

The Standards Revision Team of the Postsecondary Standards Committee:
> Richard A. Cornell
> The late Marian C. Hinz
> Robert P. Hinz
> James R. Lied
> Robert E. Spears

FORWARD

The publication by AECT of this edition of *Standards For College and University Learning Resources Programs: Technology in Instruction* marks the continuing evolution of standards for higher education learning resources support services. Because the types of support services provided by college and university Learning Resources Programs change and evolve as the result of new and emerging technologies, so must the standards by which institutions measure the effectiveness of their support services.

Building upon the previous standards, this edition includes an extensive self-study evaluation checklist to assist the staff of the Learning Resources Program in determining if their program is effective, how it can be improved, and how it compares against similar programs. New to this edition are discussions on the organizational and financial structure of the Learning Resources Program, and the professional development of the staff. This book also discusses the new technologies that are playing an increasingly prominent role in today's Learning Resources Programs.

Standards For College and University Resources Programs: Technology in Instruction not only provides a measure against which to evaluate an existing program, it also provides the basis upon which to expand services and programs. As with any set of standards, this document establishes high levels of service to which every Learning Resources Program should subscribe. It is through using this document and meeting the goals it sets forth that the Learning Resources Program will assume an increasingly important role in the educational mission of each institution.

Stanley D. Zenor
AECT Executive Director
May, 1989

INTRODUCTION

LEARNING RESOURCES PROGRAM DEFINITION

Colleges and universities are the most complex of all educational institutions. They are involved with a broad range of subject fields for both educational programs and research, information needs ranging from general to highly specialized. The services that support these educational and research needs must be encompassing.

Experience indicates that a centrally administered Learning Resources Program LRP provides the most efficient and effective means of serving all programs of the institution. Organizational schemes may include centralization of all the Learning Resources Program functions in a single unit or a combination of centralized/decentralized activities, with a central agency for general programs, and high-cost support functions for individual campus units which warrant them.

The Learning Resources Program is an academic support service that provides materials, equipment, and services to support the instructional and research programs of the institution. This document presents and discusses standards for the institution, for management, and for the program. It views each area as functionally interrelated and intrinsic to an appropriately operating Learning Resources Program. It measures each area against a unified and comprehensive standard that incorporates the following elements:

• the needs and objectives of the institution and the adequacy of the function/service in meeting them.

• the adequacy and appropriateness of personnel, equipment, and facilities for each.

• the adequacy and appropriateness of the degree of interaction of all functions/services.

These criteria for college and university LRPs are neither arbitrary nor capricious. They are the result of experience and research within institutions of varying size and type. The standards statements in Part I form the basis of program evaluation. In addition to the standards, information on levels of performance are delineated as:

minimal – defined as the lowest level of equipment, personnel, and facilities necessary to begin service in that area. This level is titled 'operational' in the management standards.

basic – defined as a second stage of development which provides an acceptable service capacity predicated on the day-to-day demands. This level is titled 'leadership' in the management standards.

advanced – defined as an expanded capacity necessary to support a sophisticated and comprehensive service. This level is titled 'innovative' in the management standards.

An institution may use these standards to determine its current quality and effectiveness. The level of performance can be used along with the quantifiable guidelines in Part II by an institution to determine its level of service capability. When this is done, we urge the evaluator to remember that the minimal, basic, and advanced levels are not discrete steps. There are gradations within and between levels that will identify the unique service capabilities of each institution. These levels represent points along a continuum of adequacy in meeting a standard to which a program may reference itself.

Unlike many other standards, this document does not specify numbers of pieces of equipment based on faculty/classroom/student size. Instead it uses the following formula: **when the Learning Resources Program cannot satisfy 95% of its requests for a given service it must grow in that area**. Such growth may be in personnel, facilities, or equipment, or in any combination of the three.

A Learning Resources Program acts as a proactive facilitator. It must bring together users, materials, and methods in order to assist users in achieving both efficiency and effective application for their particular purposes. Learning Resource Programs support the educational system in five major areas:

- Support for instructional development,
- Access to information resources and methods of teaching and learning,
- Distribution of information resources,
- Use of information resources
- Creative development of information resources.

Common to all of these areas is the responsibility for providing leadership in the innovative use of learning materials and methods.

Each Learning Resources Program is unique – molded by the parent institution's objectives, needs, and organization. Effective programs in all institutions, however, contain full and integrated support of elements of each of the above areas in varying degrees. It is no longer possible for either students, teachers, or researchers to access a full range of information on a given subject without the use of sophisticated retrieval methods. A student also cannot fully understand a subject without access to varying materials formats. Information has increased not only in complexity and volume but also in its reliance on multiple channels of communication. The Learning Resources Program must ensure that its clients have the ability and means to use all of the communications channels.

The services discussed within these standards have traditionally included such separate units as libraries, media centers, self-instructional laboratories, and audiovisual production centers, among others. Administrative and functional divisions and separations have existed between these units based on media formats or historical development. Such divisions often encourage, rather than diminish, the barriers to instructional and research support.

By examining functions rather than traditional or historical divisions, these standards outline the development of an integrated service – a service concerned with the improvement of instruction. Based solely on the user's need, such a service should provide efficient access to and delivery of information, regardless of format. These standards provide criteria by which an institution can measure its progress in reaching instructional and research needs. They also act as a guide to the development and organization of a Learning Resources Program.

PURPOSE

The purposes of these standards are:

1. To help the Learning Resources Program director determine whether the institution is effectively providing learning resources services.

2. To provide the basis for a complete self-study and analysis of the Learning Resources Program as it currently exists.

3. To give the institution information about its Learning Resources Program that indicates where it stands in relation to similar programs throughout the country.

4. To serve as a planning tool for future growth and programmatic direction.

5. To be used as an analytical tool in determining past, current, and future budget levels as well as to provide an overall qualitative measure of the Learning Resources Program's effectiveness.

SCOPE

Learning Resources Programs differ in size, complexity, and even in mission. These standards are not prescriptive, but they assume that certain base-line services are essential to the effective functioning of every academic program. Beyond these minimal levels of support, the institution must maintain services specifically designed to meet the goals of its own constituencies.

These standards do not address either the operation or the administration of a print collection. Existing standards developed by the Association of College and Research Libraries are applicable to most institutions and they should be applied as companion standards when a Learning Resources Program has responsibility for print resources. All of the functions and services described herein should be available to the institutional community. However, the unique scope and mission of each Learning Resources Program requires the judicious selection of appropriate sections of the standards when evaluating a specific program. Individual programs can only be evaluated on the basis of functions/services which are within their institutionally-defined scope and mission.

BENEFITS

Using the standards to measure the effectiveness of the Learning Resources Program will provide numerous institutional benefits beyond their basic evaluative intent. Short-range benefits will result from the intense analysis to which the institution is subjected during the self-study process. A self-study reveals the immediate status, whether positive or negative. Many problems, identified before a review team's impending arrival, are amenable to immediate corrective action. Other short-range benefits would include the following:

- professional development of the LRP Director and staff.
- increased awareness of users to LRP services.
- identification of program changes and improvements.

The standards could provide a long-range benefit to the institution in the following ways:

- improved service to faculty, staff, and students.
- important strength for faculty recruiting.
- critical recruiting tool of potential students.
- potential to maximize funds allocated to LRP (especially if numerous, separate departments comprise it).
- potential to generate revenues through sale of developed materials, development of instructional materials for other institutions, new courses, and so on.

PART I: THE STANDARDS

1.0 INSTITUTIONAL STANDARDS

It is understood that the functions and services of the LRP are to be utilized for the improvement of the institution's instructional/research programs. Support of other institutional programs is appropriate as long as it does not disrupt the primary mission of the service. If the institution requires more support, it must provide additional financial and other resources.

The emphasis and efforts of each service of the Learning Resources Program will be on quality of performance rather than on quantity. In addition to the equipment, facilities, and personnel specified for each service, the institution shall make available the general resources necessary to support the appropriate functioning of the service.

1.1. The institution shall maintain a Learning Resources Program that:
   A. is consistent with its institutional mission and goals.
   B. meets or exceeds the minimum criteria established herein.
   C. is responsive and adaptive to the changing needs of its clients.
   D. is accountable for all activities undertaken.
   E. includes access to each of the functions identified in the standards.

1.2 The institution shall establish a statement of policy for the Learning Resources Program, including its relationships to other entities of the institution. This statement shall reflect the institution's concept of the role that the Learning Resources Program plays in accomplishing the goals and objectives of the institution.

1.3 The institution shall recruit and hire the Director of the Learning Resources Program, who shall report to the chief academic officer of the institution.

1.4 The institution shall recognize that specific programs or needs may require the development of services which are beyond the scope of these standards.

1.5 The institution shall provide the Learning Resources Program with the general resources necessary for the full and appropriate functioning of its services including, but not necessarily limited to, the following:
   A. utilities, including electrical, plumbing, cooling, heating, and ventilation.
   B. general secretarial and clerical support.
   C. communications (e.g. telephone, computer services, etc.).
   D. access to record keeping services.
   E. offices, and the supplies and equipment normally necessary for proper operations.
   F. appropriate work spaces and facilities which are accessible to the handicapped (PL(94-142), safe (OSHA approved), and aesthetically conducive to work.
   G. security for the materials, equipment, and facilities.

1.6 The institution shall recognize that the primary mission of the Learning Resources Program is the support of the instructional/research programs. Support of other institutional activities will be appropriate as long as the primary mission is not interrupted or degraded, and additional support is provided to carry out such activities.

1.7 The institution shall recognize that the emphasis of the Learning Resources Program, and each of its components, will be placed on the quality, rather than the quantity, of performance.

1.8. The institution shall provide the Learning Resources Program with a budget:
   A. that is adequate to meet its role and function.
   B. that is identified separately from other institutional budgets.
   C. for which it is responsible to the institution.

1.9. The institution shall provide the director of the Learning Resources Program with:
   A. professional staff members who possess the education, training, and/or certification commensurate with their areas of responsibility.
   B. support staff adequate to meet the roles and functions of the Learning Resources Program.

1.10. The institution shall recognize and encourage:
  A. the professional status and functioning of the director and staff of the Learning Resources Program, and its components, as appropriate.
  B. the professional development of Learning Resources Program staff through supported educational opportunities both on and off campus.

1.11. The institution shall provide one or more facilities with common microcomputer systems and appropriate software available for use by students and staff. Separate facilities for administrative and instructional uses should be provided.

1.12. The institution shall assume responsibility for ensuring user compliance with relevant copyright law and software licensing agreements. A model policy for such compliance is provided within the "International Council For Computers in Education (ICEE) Document" on copyright compliance.

2.0 MANAGEMENT STANDARDS

A most critical part of this standards document is the management of the Learning Resources Program. We have taken care to provide important benchmarks to describe not only current situations, but also possible new areas for program development.

These management standards are designed to apply to single-person LRPs, as well as large multiunit programs. Each campus has its unique qualities, and it is the responsibility of the director of the Learning Resources Program to customize it to the nature of the campus and its setting.

Implicit in the management standards is the director's ability to work with a wide range of staff, administrators and users. The director should also foster the professional development of staff, of him or herself, and of the persons the Learning Resources Program serves.

The management standards address professional competence from several perspectives. They do not, however, directly consider other personnel. From an organizational viewpoint, only the director of the Learning Resources Program is responsible for the program and its resources. This person is key to the development of the Learning Resources Program. Others may be important, but without good management, the program has little chance of success.

Leadership has become a critical element in the effective implementation of a Learning Resources Program. Consequently, the management standards identify the basic level as the "Leadership Level". Often in the early stages of program development, leadership can be more important than many of the elements of the "Operational Level" which is the equivalent of "Basic Level" identified in other parts of the standards. For instance, while documenting job tasks and assignments is essential for continued operational success, new technical areas require greater attention to leadership in gathering support and motivating staff.

Learning Resources Programs are still "new" phenomena in some colleges and universities. In many cases they are not welcomed; in others they are merely tolerated. Issues of academic freedom, emphasis on writing and research, and traditional beliefs often require high levels of creative leadership to achieve excellence in instructional support service. The "Innovative Level" attempts to address management skills at this highest level. At the innovative level, the director is in the middle, often being asked to find congruency between institutional constraints and expectations on the one hand, and user's needs for service on the other.

2.1 DIRECTOR OF THE LEARNING RESOURCES PROGRAM

Purpose: To be responsible for the Learning Resources Program functions, as well as their action and direction.

2.1.1 Knowledge The director of the Learning Resources Program shall have a well-rounded in-depth knowledge of learning resources and demonstrated knowledge of management.

Operational Level (Minimum Knowledge Criteria)
The director's educational background should include an appropriate terminal degree with training in administration and management science, learning and communication theory, systems analysis and design, curriculum and instructional development, and information science. Terminal degree level shall be commensurate with that expected of faculty at the institution. Demonstrated management experience may substitute for terminal degree. Work experience includes success in a similar position at an equal or lower level. The director is familiar with institutional rules, regulations, and policies, as well as the authority structure of the institution's governance.

Leadership Level (Basic Knowledge Criteria) In addition to meeting the minimal criteria, the director continues to increase his or her knowledge of management science, learning and communications theory, systems analysis and design, curriculum and instructional development and information science. Continued increase in knowledge of communications and group dynamics is imperative.

Innovative Level (Advanced Knowledge Criteria) In addition to meeting the basic criteria, the director has in depth knowledge of some particular Learning Resources Program area of study and may be recognized nationally. Not all experts need to have narrow fields of interest, however. A wide range of subject interests with a graduate level understanding will allow for comfortable interaction with a wide variety of scholars. Either or both these should ultimately lead the director to creative new information, insights and discoveries related to the profession and to the institution.

2.1.2 Attitudes The director of the Learning Resources Program shall have high moral and ethical standards and demonstrate concern for service to users and staff.

Operational Level (Minimum Attitude Criteria) The director should be pleasant, friendly, and outgoing. He or she is loyal to the Learning Resources Program, its staff, the institution and its constituents and to the profession. The highest ethical and moral standards are applied.

Leadership Level (Basic Attitude Criteria) In addition to meeting the minimal criteria, the director's primary job focus is on the uses of the Learning Resources Program. He or she is proactive in resolving users' needs with those of the Learning Resources Program and the institution. The director is not afraid to make decisions, stand by them and accept responsibility for them. The director is also willing to take risks and clear the way for those who follow. He or she can envision the Learning Resources Program of the future and bring users, staff and institutional leaders to share that vision. He or she is self-motivated.

Innovative Level (Advanced Attitude Criteria) In addition to meeting the basic criteria, and despite the obstacles, the director retains a strong, positive outlook and remains optimistic while others doubt. The director questions and probes, often creating new relationships to find the next breakthrough.

2.1.3 Skills The director of the Learning Resources Program shall manage the various resources of the Learning Resources Program and demonstrate concern for service to users and staff.

Operational Level (Minimal Skill Criteria) The director is diplomatic and able to get along well with others. He or she reacts well to crisis situations and calms potentially harmful transactions. The director is organized, and follows and respects rules, policies and procedures of the institution and the Learning Resources Program. He or she is consistent in style and exerts firm resolution where required. He or she may participate as a faculty member in an academic program.

Leadership Level (Basic Skill Criteria) In addition to meeting the minimal criteria the director delegates authority, responsibility and assignments. He or she gets staff motivated to the task at hand. He or she creates plans that respond to user needs assessments, involves staff in the planning process and allows for contingencies in the implementation of the plan. Plans should have measurable outcomes. He or she exhibits interviewing skills, meeting and presentation skills. This person should also takes the lead in reducing tension with other institutional leaders.

Innovative Level (Advanced Skill Criteria) In addition to meeting the basic criteria this person understands and uses wisely the power of the institution to make things happen. This person is skilled to turn problems into opportunities and be inspirational for staff and others to reach high levels of performance. He or she is expert at achieving resolution of user need through others. He or she may even be able to achieve economic growth for the institution through increased revenues or reduced costs.

2.2 LEARNING RESOURCES PROGRAM INFORMATION STRUCTURE STANDARDS

Purpose: To design the information structure required to effectively meet the needs of Learning Resources Program Functions described in Program Standards.

2.2.1 Goals, Objectives The director of the Learning Resources Program shall be responsible for Learning Resources Program goals and objectives.

Operational Level (Minimal Level) Goals and objectives are determined and are available in written form at least annually.

Leadership Level (Basic Level) In addition to meeting the minimal criteria, short-term (1-3 years) goals and objectives and long range (3-5 years) goals and objectives are determined and are available in written form at least annually with a user or customer focus.

Innovative Level (Advanced Level) In addition to meeting the basic criteria, the goals of the institution, the Learning Resources Program, and the staff are congruent with meeting user's needs.

2.2.2 Plans

Operational Level (minimal Level) Daily written schedules as well as monthly calendars of events and schedules are produced to show when and where activities are to occur. Accurate scale drawings of facilities used by the Learning Resources Program are available. These plans include drawings of facilities served by the Learning Resources Program; such as classrooms, laboratories, large lecture halls, etc.

Leadership Level (Basic Level) In addition to meeting the minimal criteria, written strategic plans describe the Learning Resources Program course, direction and how goals and objectives will be met. The plan shall be reviewed annually and be updated frequently based on user needs and indicated priorities.

Innovative Level (Advanced Level) In addition to meeting the basic criteria, the strategic plan is written to adapt the Learning Resources Program's course, direction and implementation plan to the institution's own strategic plan. What a Learning Resources Program sets as its top priority may not be important or useful to the institution. When these differences and other problems are encountered, they are viewed as opportunities, not problems.

2.2.3 Organization

Operational Level (Minimal Level) There are current written job descriptions for each staff member and there is an organization chart of the Learning Resources Program.

Leadership Level (Basic Level) In addition to meeting the minimal criteria, Learning Resources Program resources are organized to maximize user needs and to eliminate barriers to resolving those needs. These resources (people, facilities, equipment, time, money, etc.) are organized to anticipate contingencies.

Innovative Level (Advanced Level) In additional to meeting the basic criteria, the Learning Resources Program is a positive influence on the organization, and is a force for changing the institution's organization of resources. An additional step would include influence on the institution's commitment of resources to resolve user or customer needs. The organization of these resources may result in economic value by increasing revenues or decreasing costs.

2.2.4 Rules, Policies, Procedures

Operational Level (Minimal Level) An up-to-date policy/procedures manual is maintained and available.

Leadership Level (Basic Level) In addition to meeting the minimal criteria, rules, policies and procedures are created and changed to minimize barriers and are flexible enough to best meet user needs. All rules, policies and procedures are written in clear language without jargon.

Innovative Level (Advanced Level) In addition to meeting the basic criteria, Learning Resources Program rules, policies and procedures are integrated with other institutional programs and with the institution as a whole. Ultimately, new standards of Learning Resources Program performance better serve not only the institution, but also the profession.

2.2.5 Communication

Operational Level (Minimal Level) Users and non-users alike can quickly identify what services are offered when, where, and how. They should also tell when changes in services will occur.

Leadership Level (Basic Level) In addition to meeting the minimal criteria, a well-trained staff receives information on user needs, adjusts to any minor changes in user needs, takes major changes to the director of the Learning Resources Program and shows or tells users how services meet their needs.

Public announcements are made frequently. Annually, a services report is made describing what services were offered, what services are needed, and what plans are being made to better serve the user. Multi-year plans are encouraged.

Training users is a positive strategy to better meet user needs and encourage the exchange of ideas between staff and user.

Innovative Level (Advanced Level) In addition to meeting the basic criteria, the service is so complete and so integrated into user activity, it is almost taken for granted. Staff assignments may even be blurred with faculty activity.

Original research on communication technology, instructional systems, et. al., is conducted.

New examples of communication technology, whether equipment or materials are seen. This may include, for example, a computer program, a new concept in 16mm motion picture projectors, or a new motion picture or video program.

Application of communication technology to solve institutional problems is also seen. An example would include participation in and design of new telephone systems to solve communications and student information needs.

2.2.6 Evaluation

Operational Level (Minimal Level) Accurate records of services delivered are maintained so that an annual record of services can be produced. Each staff member has an annual performance evaluation. Equipment, facilities and other resources are also evaluated at least once annually.

Leadership Level (Basic Level) In addition to meeting the minimal criteria, there is an annual report describing what progress has been made to reach user-focused goals and objectives, as well as what new goals and objectives are being sought.

Concerns and issues of staff, users, and other constituents are collected at least annually, but special attempts are made to identify why non-users are non-users. This evaluative information is useful to compare with the turndowns for service which also are collected.

Not only should resources be evaluated annually, but the processes (of management, decision-making, and the like) also are evaluated annually.

Innovative Level (Advanced Level) In addition to meeting the basic criteria, the Learning Resources Program conducts research in a professional and scholarly manner. Studies and experiments might be hardware-oriented, process-oriented, or deal with some aspect of information theory, communications, and so on. Evaluation techniques themselves are innovative.

The evaluation effort may be designed to identify how to lower costs or increase revenues at a Learning Resources Program level, institutional or multi-institutional level.

2.3 LEARNING RESOURCES PROGRAM FINANCIAL STRUCTURE

Purpose: To design the financial structure required to meet effectively the needs of Learning Resources Program functions described in program standards.

2.3.1 Budget

Operational Level (Minimal Level) The director of the Learning Resources Program should have sufficient time to prepare a written annual budget. The budget reflects the estimated income and expenses of the various Learning Resources Program functions. The total expenditures for learning resources are not less than 3 percent of the institution's budget for educational and general expenditures. This percentage does not include book and periodical purchases, but does include personnel, materials (film, audio tape, academic computing software, curriculum resources, et.al.) and supplies and equipment. An amount of twelve percent (12%) of the current value (see 2.3.2) of equipment and materials shall be included in the 3 percent Learning Resources Program budget. Additional funds must be appropriated for new equipment purchase. All of the budget is to be spent annually unless some savings mechanism is allowed for future use.

The budget is available for a twelve-month period and is not reduced in that period.

The financial goal of this level is to maximize the use of available resources (people, facilities, equipment, time, money, etc.) to achieve cost-efficiency.

Leadership Level (Basic Level) In addition to meeting the minimal criteria, the Learning Resources Program has a written annual financial plan and a written three-to-five year financial plan, both of which have a user focus.

The financial goal of this level is to maximize the use of funds to meet Learning Resources Program and institutional goals and objectives in a cost effective manner.

Innovative Level (Advanced Level) In addition to meeting the basic criteria, the Learning Resources Program designs creative, cost-effective strategies to offer lower costs, increased revenues or improved performance.

The financial structure should be designed to incorporate breakthrough economic strategies that create a beneficial effect for the Learning Resources Program and the entire institution. Such an example would be reaching 60 percent of a student population through communications technology design without sacrificing instructional quality. Operating funds should be enhanced by the adoption of various financial strategies, such as cooperative financial strategies within the institution, charge-back financial systems, "store" accounts, and so on. Charge-back systems, for example, are useful to match user needs (demand for services) to available resources. This "market-effect" should be considered, but there are some drawbacks. Paperwork increases and discretionary funds may not be readily available to the user. Store accounts allow you to purchase products in quantity and resell them to institutional members at lower costs.

2.3.2 Current Value - The director of the Learning Resources Program shall be responsible for the current value of the Learning Resources Program.

Operational Level (Minimal Level) A current value statement is issued annually, at the end of the fiscal year, detailing the increase (or decrease) in the book value of the Learning Resources Program. This statement shows the current value at a specific point in time. (The budget, by contrast, shows cumulative income and expense during a twelve-month period.) A positive increase shows growth in the value of the Learning Resources Program.

In addition to funds that are not part of the operating budget and that do not go to zero at the end of the fiscal year (endowment, restricted funds, income, and so on), the net value after depreciation of equipment, material collections and projects is counted. By maintaining a depreciation schedule for each item of equipment over $100, the Learning Resources Program can determine current value for the entire pool of equipment. Keeping similar records for materials that cost at least $50 and projects that cost more than $2,000 also provides relevant financial information.

While depreciation rates differ for each equipment unit, material item or project, most institutions require 12 percent of the current value of equipment and materials annually to buy replacement units. This is a general standard; and a more specific institutional amount should be calculated from the depreciation guidelines elsewhere in this book.

If new equipment is required for new programs, additional funds are made available. These same standards apply to replacement of material collections (films, audio tapes, academic computing software, curriculum materials, etc.). For higher priced items (video projectors, computer labs, and so on), a formal savings account is established in anticipation of replacement purchases.

Leadership Level (Basic Level) In addition to meeting the minimal criteria, There is a written plan to increase the current value of the Learning Resources Program. This plan reflects the best way to meet user needs. It may include increased endowments, restricted funds, outside contracts, allowable savings, archival collections, special and unique collections, and so on.

Innovative Level (Advanced Level) In addition to meeting the basic criteria, there is a strategic plan to dramatically increase the current value of both the Learning Resources Program as well as that of the institution. This plan may include economic breakthroughs for both the Learning Resources Program, institution and outside organizations, any or all of which would increase current value.

3.0 PROGRAM STANDARDS

The Program Standards are divided by functional areas of service: design and development functions, creative/production functions, distribution functions, maintenance and engineering functions.

3.1 DESIGN & DEVELOPMENT FUNCTION: INSTRUCTIONAL DESIGN

Purpose: To provide leadership and expertise in assisting members of the faculty to improve the quality and appropriateness of the teaching/learning process.

3.1.1 Each institution shall maintain a program whose primary goal is the improvement of the teaching/learning process through the appropriate development of instructional methods, materials, and other resources designed to optimize information and skills acquisition.

3.1.2 The instructional design program shall identify and use a process of systematic assessment, evaluation, materials, facilities and other resources, observed outcomes, and modification as necessary.

3.1.3 The instructional design program shall be capable of and shall offer services related to both small-scale and large-scale projects.

3.1.4 The Learning Resources Program shall be structured in such a manner, both philosophically and pragmatically, that it supports and uses the instructional design process.

3.1.5 The institution shall make provisions whereby members of the faculty engaged in instructional design programs shall have their "load" reduced to allow adequate time for full participation in the process.

Instructional Design - Minimal Criteria Level The Learning Resources Program shall have:
• the ability to undertake instructional design programs with one or two faculty members annually.
• the resources available and committed as necessary to implement outcomes of the design process.
• a commitment to assign specialists to instructional design team efforts on a part-time basis.

Instructional Design - Basic Criteria Level The Learning Resources Program shall have:
• an established instructional design office within the Learning Resources Program capable of undertaking instructional design projects.
• a commitment to provide a reduced load appropriate to

the scope of the project undertaken by the participating faculty.
• assigned specialists to the instructional design office as a scheduled part of their duties.

Instructional Design - Advanced Criteria Level The Learning Resources Program shall provide:
• an instructional design office staffed with enough designers to meet 95 percent of demand for service.
• regularly scheduled reduction in loads of the faculty who participate in instructional design projects.

3.2 FACULTY DEVELOPMENT STANDARDS

Purpose: To provide leadership and expertise in assisting members of the faculty to improve the quality and appropriateness of the teaching/learning process.

3.2.1 Each institution shall maintain a program whose primary goal is the improvement of the faculty member's ability to teach. Such a program shall incorporate, but shall not be limited to, development of the following skills:
• analysis of entering and exiting learner skills.
• test and measurement development and evaluation.
• evaluation and use of instructional materials, methods and media.
• analysis and development of instructional objectives.
• development of appropriate instructional strategies.

3.2.2 The faculty development program shall be considered as an integral part of the faculty member's workload with appropriate reductions in other activities as necessary.

Faculty Development - (Minimal Criteria) Duties may be assigned to the individual responsible for management of the Learning Resources Program or to an Instructional Developer.
The program incorporates mini-sessions, seminars, and workshops on a regularly scheduled but infrequent basis.
Faculty Development - (Basic Criteria) In addition to meeting the minimal criteria, one individual within the Learning Resources Program has primary responsibility for faculty development.
Frequently scheduled programs are offered related particularly to the faculty's instructional development programs.
Programs coordinated by/for specific academic areas are undertaken.
Faculty Development - (Advanced Criteria) In addition to meeting the basic criteria, there is a multi-person department with specific responsibility for faculty development.
Faculty development programs are undertaken for specific disciplines on a systematic basis.
Programs are offered by an interdisciplinary team of specialists.
Programs are closely tied to the instructional design program undertaken by members of the faculty.

3.3 CREATIVE/PRODUCTION STANDARDS

Purpose: To plan, prepare, and create a variety of instructional materials for specific academic uses; to assist faculty members in the development and creation of such materials.

This service, comprised of visualization, audio, and combined media, must necessarily be closely interrelated, because the combined media service relies heavily on the products and facilities of its partners. The greater the degree of segregation, either physically or administratively, the greater will be the duplication of staff, facilities, and equipment, and the greater the resulting cost to the institution.

3.3.0 There shall exist a creative production function within each Learning Resources Program consisting of, at minimum, visualization services and audio services, with combined creative services introduced at the basic criteria level.

3.3.1 Instructional systems development methodology shall be applied during production of all instructional materials, as appropriate.

3.3.2 The institution shall maintain a written policy regarding ownership of locally-produced materials.

3.3.3 Visualization Service. Visualization service exists for the creation/production of visual materials for instructional purposes.

Visualization Service (Minimal Criteria) The visualization service shall have the ability to mount materials, laminate, produce overhead transparencies, produce photographic copywork, and produce simple slides.

Visualization Services (Basic Criteria) In addition to meeting the minimal criteria, the visualization service shall have the ability to produce limited, simple art work, take and print monochrome photographs, enlarge and reduce graphics materials, duplicate photographic materials, and provide location photography.

Visualization Services (Advanced Criteria) In addition to meeting the basic criteria, the visualization service shall have the ability to produce original artwork including computer generated artwork, produce photography in specialized technical applications, and do color processing and printing.

3.3.4 Audio Service. Audio services exists to record or create audio materials for instructional use either independently or in combined creative forms.

Audio Services (Minimal Criteria) The audio service shall have the ability to perform field recording of lectures, lessons, and speeches and to duplicate audio materials.

Audio Services (Basic Criteria) In addition to meeting the minimal criteria, the audio service shall have the ability to duplicate from format to format, and to create and edit original materials.

Audio Services (Advanced Criteria) In addition to meeting the basic criteria, the audio service shall have the ability to do film sound production/recording, multi-channel audio production, and audio time-code editing. It also shall have the ability to produce broadcast-quality recordings, and have access to production music libraries.

3.3.5 Combined Creative Service. Combined Creative Services should be introduced after both visualization and audio services have reached at least the basic level. Combined Creative Services could consist of sound-slide services, sound motion picture services, or television services.

Sound-slide Services (Minimal Criteria) The combined creative services shall have the ability to produce simple slide-tape programs.

Sound-slide Services (Basic Criteria) In addition to meeting the minimal criteria, the combined creative services shall have the ability to produce simple programs involving two slide projectors, an audio track, synchronized, and dissolve controls.

Sound-slide Services (Advanced Criteria) In addition to meeting the basic criteria, the combined creative services shall have the ability to produce complex programs using more than two slide projectors, stereophonic sound, and complex program controller; use computer graphics; and produce multi-image programs.

Sound Motion Pictures (Minimal Criteria) None.

Sound Motion Pictures (Basic Criteria) Offering sound motion picture production is optional. If the service exists, however, it shall have the ability to produce 16mm motion pictures with sound.

Sound Motion Pictures (Advanced Criteria) In addition to meeting the basic criteria, the combined creative services shall have the ability to produce 16mm motion pictures with lip-sync sound.

Television (Minimal Criteria) The combined creative service shall have the ability to record and playback with a single portable television camera.

Television (Basic Criteria) In addition to meeting the minimal criteria, the combined creative services shall have the ability to produce simple two-camera in-studio programs, and to record single camera productions with simple post-production editing.

Television (Advanced Criteria) In addition to meeting the basic criteria, the combined creative services shall have the ability to produce multi-camera studio programs, produce multi-camera remote productions, and do sophisticated post-production editing using character generators, time based correctors, freeze frame and AB roll capabilities. It shall also have capability for post-production/ premastering of videotapes for the purpose of mastering videodisc, mastering by an off campus lab.

3.4 DISTRIBUTION FUNCTION

Purpose: To make available the materials, equipment, and facilities necessary for the instructional program of the institution to function at a full and appropriate level.

3.4.1 Equipment Distribution

3.4.1.1 Each Learning Resources Program shall maintain a complement of instructional technology equipment of sufficient variety and number to satisfy a minimum of 95% of the annual requests for each equipment type. When 5% of the requests for an equipment type cannot be provided, then additional numbers of the equipment type should be purchased. In order to determine when the 5% rule is applicable, records should be kept on equipment requests which cannot be filled as well as equipment requests which are filled.

3.4.1.2 Equipment shall be available to patrons in a manner that encourages and facilitates its use.

3.4.1.3 The Learning Resources Program shall provide an easy and convenient mechanism for instructing patrons in the operation of equipment.

3.4.1.4 The Learning Resources Program shall provide mechanisms for developing the skills of the patron relative to the appropriate use of equipment.

3.4.1.5 The Learning Resources Program shall maintain an equipment resource pool, centrally-housed or remotely located, that adequately meets instructional program needs.

3.4.2 Electronic Distribution Standard. Each Learning Resources Program shall provide the ability to receive and distribute electronic transmissions of information including voice, video, and data, but not necessarily limited to these.

Electronic Distribution (Minimal Criteria) One large lecture hall per campus and one classroom per instructional building are equipped with permanently installed voice, video, and data distribution equipment.

Origination and distribution of the electronic signal may occur within the immediate area, although distribution to and origination from a central campus location is preferred.

Electronic Distribution (Basic Criteria) In addition to meeting the minimal criteria, all large lecture halls and half of all classrooms are equipped to receive and originate voice, video, and data transmissions.

Origination from and distribution to the remote locations occurs from a central campus location.

A central video distribution system is available for the reception of off-air or cable electronic signals.

Electronic Distribution (Advanced Criteria) In addition to meeting the basic criteria, all classrooms, lecture halls, dormitory spaces, lounges, and conference rooms shall be equipped with distribution points for all electronic formats including interactive satellite transmission/interface.

Research and development in evolving, state-of-the-art techniques and the application thereof as appropriate (i.e. fiber optics, voice transmission) should be ongoing.

3.4.3 Microcomputer Accessibility (Distribution)

3.4.3.1 Each institution shall provide a facility with common microcomputers available for use by students and staff, including printers and sufficient software. Separate facilities for administrative and instructional uses should be provided.

Microcomputer Accessibility (Minimal Criteria) The Learning Resources Program has a central facility with equipment that is available for use by classes. This facility includes a printer.

Microcomputer Accessibility (Basic Criteria) In addition to meeting the minimal criteria, the Learning Resources Program has a checkout procedure for computer literacy materials, including hardware and software.

Microcomputer Accessibility (Advanced Criteria) In addition to meeting the basic criteria, the Learning Resources Program offers microcomputer skill classes.

3.4.3.2 The Learning Resources Program shall provide software for use in the microcomputer facilities from each of the following types of software:

- drill and practice
- tutorials
- learning games
- simulations such as problem solving and critical thinking
- word processing systems
- spreadsheet analysis
- data base generator systems
- authoring languages
- authoring systems
- graphics systems - for programming support
- graphics systems - presentation graphics
- graphics systems - Computer Assisted Drafting (CAD)
- various structured languages for programming (such as: LOGO, PASCAL, C, MODULA, and APL)
- communications software packages

3.4.3.3 At least one staff member will be sufficiently familiar with the operation of microcomputers to assist users and assist staff in planning for microcomputer usage. The consultant should do short- and long-range planning with staff for microcomputer usage.

Consultant Availability (Minimal Criteria) The Learning Resources Program has a part-time staff person available to help faculty plan their use of microcomputers.

Consultant Availability (Basic Criteria) The Learning Resources Program has one half-time individual skilled in the use of microcomputers to provide consultation and assistance for faculty and students in the use of microcomputers in regular classes and in special applications.

The microcomputer consultant provides help for students with their classwork involving the use of microcomputers.

Consultant Availability (Advanced Criteria) The Learning Resources Program has one full-time individual skilled in the use of microcomputers and instructional design to provide assistance to faculty in curricular development and integration.

3.4.4 Media Resources. This function exists to develop and maintain an active program of identification, evaluation, selection, acquisition, and control of instructional materials.

3.4.4.1 The Learning Resources Program shall have sufficient funds for maintaining and expanding its media resources collection in a planned and orderly manner.

3.4.4.2 Each institution shall maintain an active materials/resources program.

3.4.4.3 Under no circumstances shall the institution operate duplicate collection programs.

3.4.4.4 All media resources should be included in both the catalog of the academic library and the catalog of the Learning Resources Program, including any on-line catalogs of instructional resources.

3.4.4.5 It is strongly recommended that the materials/resources program be a cooperative venture between the Learning Resources Program and the library.

3.4.4.6 Preview equipment of not less than one item for each type of material within the collection shall be maintained within the immediate area of the collection.

3.4.4.7 Each media resource program shall maintain an active program of temporary acquisitions and distribution of media resources from outside sources, including rental and loan.

3.4.4.8 There shall exist a systematic and ongoing media resource inspection and maintenance procedure.

Materials Resources Distribution

3.4.4.9 The Learning Resources Program shall provide a materials distribution procedure specifically designed to distribute media resources.

3.4.4.10 Distribution shall include media resources which are a part of the Learning Resources Program's collection.

3.4.4.11 Such distribution shall endeavor to ensure that the media resources are available to users on a timely basis within the context of their instructional program.

3.4.5 Microcomputer Software Standards

3.4.5.1 The Learning Resources Program shall ensure user compliance with relevant copyright law and software licensing agreements.

3.4.5.2 There shall be a program for educating students and faculty in the evaluation of software. An organized collection of software evaluations, reviews, and periodicals containing such reviews will be maintained for use by students and faculty.

Software Evaluations (Minimal Criteria) The Learning Resources Program shall provide journals plus a representative collection of software catalogs. It shall have sample software review forms and encourage their use.

Software Evaluations (Basic Criteria) In addition to meeting the minimal criteria, the Learning Resources Program provides a systematic evaluation process for software.

Software Evaluations (Advanced Criteria) In addition to meeting basic criteria, the Learning Resources Program has an on-line searchable database of software evaluations and access to off-campus databases for similar information. Citations in the online database should include software available in the microcomputer facilities as well as reviews from the journals.

3.5 MAINTENANCE AND ENGINEERING FUNCTION

Purpose: To provide a comprehensive program of preventive maintenance and repair of equipment associated with the Learning Resources Program; to maintain the capacity to design, construct, and operate systems of equipment.

3.5.1 Each Learning Resources Program shall maintain, or have easy access to, facilities, personnel, supplies, and equipment necessary to repair equipment.

3.5.2 Each Learning Resources Program shall provide routine maintenance checks on all equipment items on a regular and scheduled basis.

3.5.3 Each Learning Resources Program shall have on staff individuals qualified and trained to operate each different type and system under the jurisdiction of the Learning Resources Program.

Maintenance and Engineering (Minimal Criteria) The Learning Resources Program shall contract for services with an agency specializing in the repair of equipment, shall have a system of preventive maintenance (including inspection following use) for all equipment, and shall have a budget adequate for all repair of all items as necessary.

Maintenance and Engineering (Basic Criteria) In addition to meeting the minimal criteria, the Learning Resources Program shall have a maintenance and repair facility equipped with appropriate tools, test equipment, manuals and supplies to perform simple repairs; shall have a qualified technician capable of designing, maintaining and operating simple equipment systems.

Maintenance and Engineering (Advanced Criteria) In addition to meeting the basic criteria, the Learning Resources Program shall have an advanced maintenance and repair facility equipped with sophisticated electronic test equipment adequate to maintain and repair all equipment types, shall have technicians capable of repairing all equipment types, plus the designing, installation, and operation of complex equipment systems.

PART II: SELF-STUDY RESOURCES

INTRODUCTION TO THE SELF-STUDY RESOURCES

This section of the standards, new to this edition, is based on input from several intensive reviews of Learning Resources Programs. These procedures are meant to serve as guidelines on how to conduct a self-study. Each institution should select the procedures which are appropriate to the institution. All the suggested procedures have been used, and all have proved successful. We anticipate that the evaluation of a comprehensive Learning Resources Program will involve as many of these resources as is possible and practical.

RECOMMENDED SELF-STUDY PROCEDURES

The following self-study format has been used successfully at several institutions and is recommended. The use of outside consultant(s) in the self-study process is advised. The consultant(s) should work with campus Learning Resources Program professionals to guide their self-study effort and produce a summary evaluation of the Learning Resources Program. The choice of outside consultant should be limited to people knowledgeable about the Standards. The AECT Central Office can help you locate individuals recommended as consultants. The use of an outside consultant has several advantages. It ensures that the standards are being applied in the manner intended. It also adds a level of objectivity to the study that is not possible when only individuals from within your institution are involved. The external credibility added by outside consultants encourages the acceptance of the results of the study at the institution. The following is a list of activities to follow in conducting an assisted self-study.

1. Identify and involve an outside consultant in the study as planning begins.

2. Meet with the outside consultant to plan components of the study.

3. Completion of the Self-Study Narrative and Checklist contained in this section. These two instruments will provide a comprehensive internal evaluation of your staff's perception of the status of the Learning Resources Program. It will also provide a basis for comparison with the consultant's external perception of the Learning Resources Program.

4. Have the university community complete a User Learning Resources Program Evaluation Instrument. A sample User Evaluation Instrument is contained in this document. With the assistance of the consultant, you should adapt it to your own institution and distribute it to the entire university community. Compare the findings to the results of the internal self-study instrument for consistency. The university's perception of the value and need for services now provided (or to be provided) by the Learning Resources Program is very important to the continued success of the Learning Resource Program.

5. Schedule on-site visits by the consultants. During these visits the consultants should interview key administrators and faculty on the Learning Resources Program. They should also interview all employees of the Learning Resources Program individually. These interviews are an effective mechanism for comparing on-campus perceptions of the Learning Resources Program to the internal perceptions of the Learning Resources Program staff.

6. Develop a resource file for use by the consultants. This file should contain a compilation of pertinent Learning Resources Program documents for the last three to four years. Pertinent documents include:
- budgets
- annual reports
- goal statements
- long-range planning documents
- current position descriptions
- proposals for new or innovative services
- copies of brochures and forms used in daily operation
- summaries of type and amount of services provided.

7. Once you have completed all these phases, the consultant writes a final evaluation of the Learning Resources Program based on all previously gathered data, making recommendations as necessary.

8. A suggested interval for conducting such a self-study is every five to seven years.

LEARNING RESOURCES PROGRAM SELF-STUDY CHECKLIST & QUANTITATIVE GUIDELINES

The following checklists are designed to assist in the identifying the effectiveness and level of the institution's Learning Resources Program. In order to complete these checklists you must have a copy of the standards to work with.

1.0 INSTITUTIONAL CHECKLIST

For each standard listed place a check mark on the appropriate line if the institution, in your judgment, meets or exceeds the standard. Place no check if any part of the standard is not met totally. Total score may be obtained by adding the numbers in parentheses for each item checked. (Note: the numbers to the left of each item refer to standards listed in main text of this document.)

1.1.A   is consistent with mission_____(5)

1.1.B   exceeds minimum scope_____(3)

1.1.C   respond to change_____(5)

1.1.D   is accountable_____(5)

1.5   has general resources_____(5)

1.6   recognizes primary role_____(2)

1.7   emphasizes quality_____(2)

1.8.A   has adequate budget_____(5)

1.8.B   has separate budget_____(3)

1.9   provides adequate staffing_____(5)

1.10.A   accords professional status_____(5)

1.10.B   supports professional development_____(5)

Total general score_____of possible 50

2.0 MANAGEMENT CHECKLIST

Instructions: Circle the appropriate number of points for each statement. Add or delete items to customize the instruments. Comments are encouraged.

2.1 DIRECTOR OF LEARNING RESOURCES PROGRAM

Purpose: To be responsible for the Learning Resources Program management functions, as well as their action and direction.

2.1.1 Knowledge (includes facts, data, professional information, recorded experiences, etc.)

	Points	Comments
Operational Level (Minimal Criteria)		
Has an appropriate terminal degree.	0 1	
Has extensive, prior work experience.	0 1	
Has prior success as a manager.	0 1	
Has prior accomplishments, awards, scholarly work, etc.	0 1	
Has knowledge of rules, policies and authority structure.	0 1	
Leadership Level (Basic Criteria)		
Has a personal program of continuing education and development.	0 1 2 3	
Actively reads current journals and news media.	0 1 2 3	
Shows knowledge of group dynamics.	0 1 2 3	
Continually works toward improving communication skills.	0 1 2 3	
Innovative Level (Advanced Criteria)		
Has an in-depth knowledge of several topics related to the Learning Resources Program.	0 1 2 3 4 5	
Has received national recognition for work.	0 1 2 3 4 5	
Is on the "cutting edge" of several topics related to the Learning Resources Program.	0 1 2 3 4 5	
Creates new information in some media form, such as book, or film, or video program.	0 1 2 3 4 5	

2.1.2 Attitudes (includes personal approach to world, values, feelings, overt behaviors, expressions, expectations, cognitive styles, etc.)

	Points	Comments
Operational Level (Minimal Criteria)		
Is genuinely friendly, pleasant and outgoing.	0 1	
Treats Learning Resources Program staff and customers with courtesy and consistency.	0 1	
Is honest, ethical and loyal to self, staff, organization and profession.	0 1	
Leadership Level (Basic Criteria)		
Maintains a user-focus.	0 1 2 3	
Has a proactive involvement with staff and customers.	0 1 2 3	
Is self-motivated.	0 1 2 3	
Makes decisions and does not avoid them.	0 1 2 3	
Is willing to take risks.	0 1 2 3	
Has visions or plans to see the Learning Resources Program progress.	0 1 2 3	

	Points	Comments
Has record of accomplishments in this position	0 1 2 3	

Innovative Level (Advanced Criteria)

	Points	Comments
Maintains a positive outlook but continues to probe for better ways.	0 1 2 3 4 5	
Is firm in resolution, but keeps flexible, creative.	0 1 2 3 4 5	
Has determination and drive to see desired results.	0 1 2 3 4 5	
Has wide network of support.	0 1 2 3 4 5	

2.1.3. Skills (includes application of knowledge and attitudes, habits, cognitive styles, "how to do it", etc.)

	Points	Comments

Operational Level (Minimal Criteria)

Reacts well to current situations, problems.	0 1	
Exhibits organization, consistency in day-to-day operations.	0 1	
Is diplomatic in dealing with staff and customers.	0 1	
Instructs in an academic program.	0 1	
Follows rules, policies, procedures.	0 1	

Leadership Level (Basic Criteria)

Delegates responsibility.	0 1 2 3	
Has regular assessments of customer needs, staff needs.	0 1 2 3	
Plans for nearly everything using short-and-long range plans.	0 1 2 3	
Connects control to plans (measurable outcomes).	0 1 2 3	
Can get staff motivated, challenged and ready.	0 1 2 3	
Remains adaptable, flexible for contingencies.	0 1 2 3	
Minimized duplication of campus services.	0 1 2 3	

Innovative Level (Advanced Criteria)

Deals well with the subtlety of organizational politics.	0 1 2 3 4 5	
Makes the power of the organization work for the Learning Resources Program.	0 1 2 3 4 5	
Remains inspirational to staff in spite of problems.	0 1 2 3 4 5	
Achieves economic growth for the organization.	0 1 2 3 4 5	
Achieves creative solutions to do things better, faster and cheaper.	0 1 2 3 4 5	
Seeks cooperative solutions.	0 1 2 3 4 5	

2.2 LEARNING RESOURCES PROGRAM INFORMATION STRUCTURE

Purpose: To design the information structure required to effectively meet needs of Learning Resources Program functions.

2.2.1 Goals, Objectives

	Points	Comments

Operational Level (Minimal Criteria)

Goals and objectives are written annually.	0 1	

Leadership Level (Basic Criteria)

Goals and objectives are written for one-year, and three-to-five year time periods with a user or customer focus.	0 1 2 3	

Innovative Level (Advanced Criteria)

Goals and objectives are written to match organizational goals with Learning Resources Program personnel goals.	0 1 2 3 4 5	

2.2.2. Plans

	Points	Comments
Operational Level (Minimal Criteria)		
Daily written schedules are produced.	0 1	
Monthly calendars and schedules are produced.	0 1	
Accurate same-scale floor plans are available for all facilities served by the Learning Resources Program.	0 1	
Leadership Level (Basic Criteria)		
Written strategic plans are produced annually.	0 1 2 3	
User needs are assessed annually.	0 1 2 3	
User needs are part of strategic plans.	0 1 2 3	
Innovative Level (Advanced Criteria)		
Strategic plans are written in high to low organizational priority order.	0 1 2 3 4 5	
Problems are seen as opportunities.	0 1 2 3 4 5	

2.2.3 Organization

	Points	Comments
Operational Level (Minimal Criteria)		
Current, written job descriptions are available for all staff.	0 1	
A current organizational chart is available.	0 1	
Leadership Level (Basic)		
Resources are organized to maximize user needs.	0 1 2 3	
Minimal road blocks to solving user's needs exist.	0 1 2 3	
Resources are organized to to anticipate contingencies.	0 1 2 3	
Innovative Level (Advanced Criteria)		
Offers a proactive influence on Learning Resources Program in the institution's structure.	0 1 2 3 4 5	
Offers a proactive influence on the institution's organization to better serve users or customers.	0 1 2 3 4 5	
Offers dramatic or innovative change in Learning Resources Program organization to create economic advantage for the institution.	0 1 2 3 4 5	

2.2.4 Rules, Policies, Procedures

	Points	Comments
Operational Level (Minimal Criteria)		
An up-to-date policy/procedure manual is maintained and available.	0 1	
Leadership Level (Basic Criteria)		
Policies are created or changed to minimize roadblocks and solve user needs.	0 1 2 3	
Policies and procedures are flexible to best meet user needs.	0 1 2 3	
Users can easily understand policies and procedures.	0 1 2 3	
Innovative Level (Advanced Criteria)		
Has successful experience in coordinating policies and procedures.	0 1 2 3 4 5	
Established new standards of performance, such as this document.	0 1 2 3 4 5	

2.2.5 Communication

	Points	Comments

Operational Level (Minimal Criteria)
An up-to-date brochure and/or catalog of services and materials
    is available to users.　　0 1
Users can easily find out when changes in services offered occur.　　0 1

Leadership Level (Basic Criteria)
Services are targeted to meet specific user needs.　　0 1 2 3
Staff are trained to respond effectively to user needs.　　0 1 2 3
Public announcements and publicity occur frequently.　　0 1 2 3
Annual written communication plans are made.　　0 1 2 3
Multi-year written communication plans are made.　　0 1 2 3
User training is planned, promoted, provided, and evaluated.　　0 1 2 3

Innovative Level (Advanced Criteria)
Learning Resources Program agenda becomes transparent
    to all institutional activities.　　0 1 2 3 4 5
Original research in instructional learning resource programs is done.　　0 1 2 3 4 5
New professional communication vehicles are created.　　0 1 2 3 4 5
Communication technology is used to solve complex institutional
    problems with positive economic and mission effects.　　0 1 2 3 4 5

2.2.6 Evaluation

	Points	Comments

Operational Level (Minimal Criteria)
Records of services delivered are maintained.　　0 1
An annual report is issued and available to staff.　　0 1
Each staff member has an annual performance appraisal.　　0 1
Nearly all resources are evaluated annually.　　0 1

Leadership Level (Basic Criteria)
The annual report describes what progress has been made
    to reach goals, objectives, as well as what new goals
    and objectives to seek.　　0 1 2 3
Issues and concerns are collected annually from staff and users.　　0 1 2 3
Non-users are identified.　　0 1 2 3
Non-users are measured against the 5% turndown for services.　　0 1 2 3
Nearly all processes are evaluated annually.　　0 1 2 3

Innovative Level (Advanced Criteria)
Innovative evaluation techniques are used.　　0 1 2 3 4 5
Learning Resources Program research is conducted and
    professionally documented.　　0 1 2 3 4 5
Successful economic advantages for the institution have
    resulted from Learning Resources Program evaluation efforts.　　0 1 2 3 4 5

2.3 LEARNING RESOURCES PROGRAM FINANCIAL STRUCTURE

Purpose: To design the financial structure required to meet effectively the needs of Learning Resources Program management functions.

2.3.1 Budget

	Points	Comments
Operational Level (Minimal Criteria)		
A written Learning Resources Program budget of expense and income is prepared annually.	0 1	
One-hundred percent of the Learning Resources Program budget is spent annually.	0 1	
Funds are maximized to the use of available resources (cost efficiency).	0 1	
Leadership Level (Basic Criteria)		
The Learning Resources Program has a one-year and three-to-five year financial plan.	0 1 2 3	
The financial plan reflects user or customer needs.	0 1 2 3	
Funds are maximized to goals and objectives (cost effectiveness).	0 1 2 3	
Innovative Level (Advanced Criteria)		
There are documented examples of creative financial strategies.	0 1 2 3 4 5	
Breakthrough economic strategies create a beneficial effect for the entire institution.	0 1 2 3 4 5	
Cooperative financial strategies are employed.	0 1 2 3 4 5	

2.3.2 Current Value

	Points	Comments
Operational Level (Minimal Criteria)		
A written current value statement is issued annually.	0 1	
A depreciation schedule for the equipment inventory is available and used.	0 1	
A depreciation schedule for the equipment inventory is available and used.	0 1	
A depreciation schedule for material productions and instructional design projects is available and used.	0 1	
Leadership Level (Basic Criteria)		
A written plan exists to increase the Learning Resources Program current value.	0 1 2 3	
The current value is increased and developed to reflect the best way to meet user needs.	0 1 2 3	
Innovative Level (Advanced Criteria)		
A strategic plan to dramatically increase the Learning Resources Program and the institution's current value is available.	0 1 2 3 4 5	
Using current value, economic breakthroughs are achieved for the Learning Resources Program and the Institution.	0 1 2 3 4 5	

MANAGEMENT CHECKLIST SCORE PROFILE

Evaluation of _____

Date of _____

	Operational Level (Minimal)	Leadership Level (Basic)	Innovative Level (Advanced)
2.1 DIRECTOR OF LEARNING RESOURCES PROGRAM			
2.1.1 Knowledge	___pts.(0-5)	___pts.(0-12)	___pts.(0-20)
2.1.2 Attitude	___pts.(0-3)	___pts.(0-21)	___pts.(0-20)
2.1.3 Skills	___pts.(0-5)	___pts.(0-21)	___pts.(0-30)
Totals	___pts.(0-13)	___pts.(0-54)	___pts.(0-70)
2.2 LEARNING RESOURCES PROGRAM INFORMATION STRUCTURE			
2.2.1 Goals, Objectives	___pts.(0-1)	___pts.(0-3)	___pts.(0-15)
2.2.2 Plans	___pts.(0-3)	___pts.(0-9)	___pts.(0-10)
2.2.3 Organization	___pts.(0-2)	___pts.(0-9)	___pts.(0-15)
2.2.4 Rules, Policies	___pts.(0-1)	___pts.(0-9)	___pts.(0-10)
2.2.5 Communication	___pts.(0-2)	___pts.(0-18)	___pts.(0-20)
2.2.6 Evaluation	___pts.(0-4)	___pts.(0-15)	___pts.(0-15)
Totals	___pts.(0-13)	___pts.(0-63)	___pts.(0-85)
2.3 LEARNING RESOURCES PROGRAM FINANCIAL STRUCTURE			
2.3.1 Budget	___pts.(0-3)	___pts.(0-9)	___pts.(0-15)
2.3.2 Current Value	___pts.(0-3)	___pts.(0-6)	___pts.(0-10)
Totals	___pts.(0-6)	___pts.(0-15)	___pts.(0-25)

MANAGEMENT CHECKLIST

CUMULATIVE TOTALS ___pts.(0-32)   ___pts.(0-132)   ___pts.(0-180)

COMBINED TOTAL   (Operational, Leadership, and Innovative)

_____ pts. (0-344)

3.0 PROGRAM CHECKLIST

3.1 INSTRUCTIONAL DEVELOPMENT STANDARDS

Existing clearly defined program_____(25)
Reduced Faculty Load_____(25)

LEVEL	PERSONNEL	FACILITIES	EQUIPMENT
Minimal	Person with professional training in instructional development at master's level.	None required.	None required.
Basic	Professional with doctoral degree in instructional development or related field, plus clerical assistance.	Private office with adjoining conference and work space.	Additional office equipment; access to computer and production equipment.
Advanced	Additional instructional developer(s) as needed, with clerical assistance, to meet 95 percent of demand for service.	One office space per individual.	Additional office equipment as needed.

3.2 FACULTY DEVELOPMENT STANDARDS

LEVEL	PERSONNEL	FACILITIES	EQUIPMENT
Minimal	Person with professional training in college teaching, or at least 5 years experience as a college teacher.	Part-time classroom or similar meeting space.	None required.
Basic	Professional with doctoral degree in higher education, college teaching, or a doctoral degree in an academic discipline and at least 10 years experience as a college teacher, plus clerical assistance.	Private office with adjoining conference and work space.	Access to computer terminal.

LEVEL	PERSONNEL	FACILITIES	EQUIPMENT
Advanced	Additional faculty developer(s) as needed to meet 95 percent of demand for service, plus one clerical assistant for every three developers, plus one graduate assistant per developer as available.	One office per individual, plus facility for theatre-style presentations.	Additional computer access facilities and equipment, plus equipment for theatre-style presentations.

SCORING CHART FOR INSTRUCTIONAL DEVELOPMENT & FACULTY DEVELOPMENT

LEVEL	PERSONNEL	FACILITIES	EQUIPMENT
Minimum	(5)	—	—
Basic	(15)	(5)	(3)
Advanced	(25)	(15)	(5)

TOTAL DEVELOPMENT SCORE_____ (0-95)

3.3 CREATIVE/PRODUCTION STANDARDS

For 3.3.1 and 3.3.2, place a checkmark on the appropriate line if the institution, in your judgment, meets, or exceeds the standard.

3.3.1 Instructional development methodology applied during production of instructional materials _____ (10)

3.3.2 Institution maintains written policy regarding ownership of locally-produced instructional materials._____(10)

3.3.3 Visualization Services

Check One:
Advanced Criteria Met_____ (10)
Basic Criteria Met_____ (6)
Minimal Criteria Met_____ (2)

LEVEL	PERSONNEL	FACILITIES	EQUIPMENT
Minimal	Person with professional training or experience in materials production.	Workroom with tables.	Dry-mount press, light table, laminator, paper cutter, and transparency maker.
Basic	Graphic artist/photographer with professional training, plus darkroom assistant.	Art production studio, darkroom, and finishing area.	Drafting tables, system for lettering, copystand and cameras; plus equipment for photo printing, finishing, and mounting.

| Advanced | Graphic designer, photographer, and cinematographer with professional training, plus production, darkroom, and finishing technician(s). | Art studio, photo studio, cinema studio, and computer generated graphics. | Motion photography, color processing, and animation equipment |

SCORING CHART FOR VISUALIZATION SERVICE STANDARDS

LEVEL	PERSONNEL	FACILITIES	EQUIPMENT
Minimum	(1)	(1)	(5)
Basic	(10)	(5)	(10)
Advanced	(25)	(15)	(15)

TOTAL VISUALIZATION SERVICE SCORE _____ (0-65)

3.3.4 Audio Service

Check One:
Advanced Criteria Met_____ (10)
Basic Criteria Met_____ (6)
Minimal Criteria Met_____ (2)

LEVEL	PERSONNEL	FACILITIES	EQUIPMENT
Minimal	Part-time assistance as required.	None required.	Audio recorders and related equipment.
Basic	Audio technician or equivalent.	Audio studio and control room.	Turntables, tape decks, audio mixers and related equipment, and audio disc.
Advanced	Full-time audio production professional(s) as needed to meet 95% of audio production requests.	Expanded audio studio.	Film sound equipment and upgraded broadcast audio system.

SCORING CHART FOR AUDIO SERVICE STANDARDS

LEVEL	PERSONNEL	FACILITIES	EQUIPMENT
Minimal	(0)		(2)
Basic	(3)	(5)	(5)
Advanced	(10)	(10)	(10)

TOTAL AUDIO SERVICE SCORE _____ (0-40)

3.3.5 Combined Creative Services: Slide-Tape

Check One:
Advanced Criteria Met_____ (10)
Basic Criteria Met_____ (6)
Minimal Criteria Met_____ (2)

LEVEL	PERSONNEL	FACILITIES	EQUIPMENT
Minimal	Work handled by personnel from visualization or audio service.	Facilities provided by visualization or audio service.	Equipment provided by visualization and audio service.
Basic	Part-time slide-tape professional as needed.	Work space, assembly/ production room, and viewing area.	Two slide projectors, audiotape recorder/ synchronizer, and dissolve controller.
Advanced	Professional slide-tape producer(s) as needed to meet 95% of requests for service.	Viewing area, facility for theater style presentations.	Additional projection control and audio equipment, and multi-image capability.

SCORING CHART FOR COMBINED CREATIVE SERVICES: SLIDE-TAPE STANDARDS

LEVEL	PERSONNEL	FACILITIES	EQUIPMENT
Minimal	—	—	—
Basic	(10)	(1)	(5)
Advanced	(10)	(5)	(10)

TOTAL COMBINED CREATIVE SERVICES: SLIDE-TAPE SCORE_____ (0-35)

3.3.5 Combined Creative Services: Sound Motion Picture

Check One:
Advanced Criteria Met_____ (10)
Basic Criteria Met_____ (6)
Minimal Criteria Met_____ (2)

LEVEL	PERSONNEL	FACILITIES	EQUIPMENT
Minimal	None required.	None required.	None required.
Basic	Part-time cinematographer.	Editing facility.	Cameras and editing equipment.
Advanced	Producer shared with slide-tape service.	Shared cinema studio, plus sound editing and studio viewing area.	Animation equipment.

SCORING CHART FOR COMBINED CREATIVE SERVICES: SOUND MOTION PICTURE

LEVEL	PERSONNEL	FACILITIES	EQUIPMENT
Minimal	—	—	—
Basic	(5)	(5)	(5)
Advanced	(10)	(10)	(10)

TOTAL COMBINED CREATIVE SERVICES: SOUND MOTION PICTURE SCORE _____ (0-40)

3.3.5 Combined Creative Services: Television

Check One:
Advanced Criteria Met _____ (10)
Basic Criteria Met _____ (6)
Minimal Criteria Met _____ (2)

LEVEL	PERSONNEL	FACILITIES	EQUIPMENT
Minimal	Part-time technician as necessary to fill 95% of requests for service.	Storage Space.	Portable equipment.
Basic	Television producer(s) as necessary to fill 95% of requests for service.	Television studio control room complex.	Studio equipment including two or more cameras, film chain, audio equipment, and basic post production editing equipment, plus remote production capabilities.
Advanced	Additional professionally trained production crew plus television staff as needed, including technicians, producers, writers, and engineers.	Television studio complex plus remote production and transmission capability.	Remote multicamera system, postproduction editing with character generator and AB roll capability, frame storage, and videodisc.

SCORING CHART FOR COMBINED CREATIVE SERVICES: TELEVISION STANDARDS

LEVEL	PERSONNEL	FACILITIES	EQUIPMENT
Minimal	—	—	—
Basic	(10)	(10)	(15)
Advanced	(25)	(20)	(20)

TOTAL COMBINED CREATIVE SERVICES: TELEVISION SCORE _____ 0-75)

3.4 DISTRIBUTION STANDARDS

3.4.1 Equipment Distribution

3.4.1.1   95% of requests satisfied_____(10)
3.4.1.2   Patron Instruction_____(5)
3.4.1.3   Patron Skill Development_____(5)
3.4.1.4   Equipment Resources:

           Advanced Criteria Met_____(15)
           Basic Criteria Met_____(10)
           Minimum Criteria Met_____(5)

LEVEL	PERSONNEL	FACILITIES	EQUIPMENT
Minimal	Distribution clerk and part-time assistant(s).	Office, storage, and equipment marshalling areas.	Equipment that is appropriate and adequate to meet 95% of requests for service.
Basic	Scheduling assistant as needed to provide service.	Expanded areas for offices, storage, and equipment.	Delivery vehicles suited to institution.
Advanced	Additional professional(s) for distribution services as needed, plus trained operators.	Expanded areas for staff and delivery personnel, including remote center distribution capability.	_____

SCORING CHART FOR EQUIPMENT DISTRIBUTION STANDARDS

LEVEL	PERSONNEL	FACILITIES	EQUIPMENT
Minimal	(5)	(5)	—
Basic	(10)	(10)	—
Advanced	(25)	(15)	—

TOTAL EQUIPMENT DISTRIBUTION SCORE _____ (0-75)

3.4.2 Electronic Distribution

Check One:
Advanced Criteria Met_____ (15)
Basic Criteria Met_____ (10)
Minimal Criteria Met_____ (5)

LEVEL	PERSONNEL	FACILITIES	EQUIPMENT
Minimal	Electronic technician as needed.	Local or central (remote) distribution area.	Videotape recorders as needed, monitors, and head-end equipment.
Basic	Additional electronic professional(s) as needed	Central electronic distribution/ reception functionally located with television production control.	Institutional and video distribution, plus satellite down-link capabilities.
Advanced	Electronic engineer(s) and technicians as needed.	Expanded area.	Satellite up-link capabilities plus remote interconnection.

SCORING CHART FOR ELECTRONIC DISTRIBUTION STANDARDS

LEVEL	PERSONNEL	FACILITIES	EQUIPMENT
Minimal	(1)	(2)	(10)
Basic	(1)	(5)	(20)
Advanced	(10)	(10)	(25)

TOTAL ELECTRONIC DISTRIBUTION SCORE _____ (0-60)

3.4.3 Microcomputer Accessibility

3.4.3.1 Microlab:

    Advanced Criteria Met_____ (15)
    Basic Criteria Met _____ (10)
    Minimal Criteria Met _____ (5)

3.4.3.2 Microcomputer Software Accessibility_____ (5)
3.4.3.3 Microcomputer Consultant::

    Advanced Criteria Met_____ (15)
    Basic Criteria Met_____ (10)
    Minimal Criteria Met_____ (5)

LEVEL	PERSONNEL	FACILITIES	HARDWARE/SOFTWARE
Minimal	One laboratory assistant per facility plus access to computer specialist.*	Climate-controlled facilities (classroom, laboratory, or combination with office and storage space) with separate power circuits, plus controlled security, static control, and availability of discs, printer supplies such as ribbons, and printer paper	Student microcomputer systems with single disc drive and graphics capability, instructor station** with 2 disc drives, printer interface, and printer; software programs; access to off-campus databases or computer from the microcomputer facility. All machines must have enough memory to run purchased software packages.

LEVEL	PERSONNEL	FACILITIES	EQUIPMENT
Basic	Two laboratory assistants per facility, plus access to computer specialist* and secretary.	Minimal facilities with additional offices and rooms for training sessions, plus checkout procedure for computer literacy materials and hardware.	Minimal level hardware/software, plus one printer and interface for every five student systems; two of each of several brands of microcomputer systems to expand exposure to a variety of brands; multiple copies of software proportional to increased numbers of systems; local network in facility so users can share files, software, or peripherals; student access to computers or databases from locations other than computer facilities. All machines should have 25% more memory than at minimal level.
Advanced	Two or more laboratory assistants per facility, plus one full-time computer specialist*/programmer, one full-time secretary and one laboratory administrator.	Basic facilities, plus electronic security system, power conditioning equipment, and skill classes for faculty and students.	Basic level hardware/software, plus interactive video equipment, robots, speech synthesizers, graphics tablets, light pens, music synthesis adapters, plotters, video digitizers, and other current developments; a variety of brands of each kind of software; hardwire lines from facility to other locations for resource sharing to allow remote-site use of local area network; on-line messaging such as bulletin board system or computer conferencing for access by students and faculty; increased memory as needed to run new software.

* The computer specialist typically would be the laboratory manager, with responsibility included for coordinating hardware maintenance and hardware/software replacement.

** Instructors should have one student contact hour per week for beginning users and two student contact hours per week for advanced users.

SCORING CHART FOR MICROCOMPUTER ACCESSIBILITY STANDARDS

LEVEL	PERSONNEL	FACILITIES	EQUIPMENT
Minimal	(5)	(5)	(5)
Basic	(10)	(7)	(10)
Advanced	(20)	(10)	(20)

TOTAL MICROCOMPUTER ACCESSIBILITY SCORE _____ (0-90)

3.4.4 Media Resources

3.4.4.1	Existing Permanent Collection_____	(5)
3.4.4.3	Non-duplication of services_____	(3)
3.4.4.4	Common Public Catalogs_____	(5)
3.4.4.5	Cooperation with Library_____	(10)
3.4.4.6	Preview Equipment_____	(5)
3.4.4.7	Temporary Acquisitions _____	(5)
3.4.4.8	Materials/Resources Maintenance_____	(5)
3.4.4.11	Materials/Resources Availability_____	(5)

(Check One):
Advanced Criteria Met_____ (25)
Basic Criteria Met_____ (15)
Minimal Criteria Met_____ (5)
Expansion Potential_____ (5)

LEVEL	PERSONNEL	FACILITIES	EQUIPMENT
Minimal	Staff member(s) as needed.	Climate-controlled materials storage and checkout facility, including preview and viewing.	Film inspection equipment and preview equipment for all formats in use.
Basic	Professional staff member(s) assistant(s) as needed.	Additional space as needed.	Film and video inspection and maintenance equipment.
Advanced	Technical staff member(s) and assistant(s) as needed.	Additional space as needed.	Additional equipment as needed.

SCORING CHART FOR MEDIA RESOURCES STANDARDS

LEVEL	PERSONNEL	FACILITIES	EQUIPMENT
Minimal	(10	(10)	(5)
Basic	(20)	(10)	(5)
Advanced	(30)	(10)	(5)

TOTAL MEDIA RESOURCES SCORE _____ (0-118)

3.4.5 Microcomputer Software

Check One:
Advanced Criteria Met_____ (15)
Basic Criteria Met_____ (10)
Minimal Criteria Met_____ (5)
Total Microcomputing Software Score_____ of 15 possible.

3.5 MAINTENANCE AND ENGINEERING STANDARDS

Regularly Scheduled Maintenance_____ (10)
Access to System Designer_____ (2)
Systems Operators_____ (5)

(Check one):
Advanced Criteria Met _____ (10)
Basic Criteria Met _____ (6)
Minimal Criteria Met _____ (2)

LEVEL	PERSONNEL	FACILITIES	EQUIPMENT
Minimal	Part-time technician(s) as needed.	Small repair shop.	Basic tools and test equipment.
Basic	Technician, plus field assistants for cleaning and inspection.	Expanded repair shop.	Specialized tools and test equipment.
Advanced	Engineers and technicians as needed to meet 95% of requests for service.	Expanded shop, office, storage, and construction areas.	Sophisticated electronic test equipment, plus equipment for device fabrication.

SCORING CHART FOR MAINTENANCE AND ENGINEERING STANDARDS

LEVEL	PERSONNEL	FACILITIES	EQUIPMENT
Minimal	(5)	(5)	(5)
Basic	(10)	(7)	(10)
Advanced	(20)	(10)	(20)

TOTAL MAINTENANCE AND ENGINEERING SCORE _____ (0-77)

SUMMARY SHEET

Use this summary sheet to tabulate your overall point score from the previous checklist sections.

STANDARDS	Points Received	Points Possible
1.0 INSTITUTIONAL TOTAL	_____	50
2.0 Management Scores:		
2.1 Director of Learning Resources Program	_____	70
2.2 Information Structure	_____	85
2.3 Financial Structure	_____	180
3.0 PROGRAM STANDARDS:		
3.1/3.2 Development	_____	95
3.3 Creative/Production:		
3.3.1 Ins. Dev. Use	_____	10
3.3.2 Ownership policy	_____	10
3.3.3 Visualization	_____	65
3.3.4 Audio	_____	40
3.3.5 Combined: Slide Tape	_____	35
3.3.5 Combined: Sound Motion Picture	_____	40
3.3.5 Combined: Television	_____	75
3.4 Distribution		
3.4.1 Equipment Distribution	_____	75
3.4.2 Electronic Distribution	_____	60
3.4.3 Microcomputer Accessibility	_____	90
3.4.4 Media Resources	_____	118
3.4.5 Microcomputer Software	_____	15
3.5 Maintenance and Engineering	_____	77
TOTAL SCORE:	_____	1190

CHECKLIST SUMMARY RATINGS

1000 to 1128	Superior Services
900 to 1000	Advanced Services
800 to 899	Low Advanced Services
700 to 799	High Basic Services
600 to 699	Basic Services
500 to 599	Low Basic Services
400 to 499	High Minimum Services
300 to 399	Minimum Services
299 or less	Below Minimal Services

LEARNING RESOURCES PROGRAM SELF-STUDY NARRATIVE

A narrative developed evaluating the role and scope of Learning Resources Program services is an important part of any self-study and should not be overlooked. The narrative should be developed in response to the questions asked in this narrative section. The resulting narrative will outline the major points in the standards in relation to the local Learning Resources Program.

PURPOSES:
1. What are the objectives of the Learning Resources Program?
2. How do they support the institution's objectives?
3. How were these objectives determined?
   3.1 Who overtly, covertly, sets policy?
   3.2 How, by whom, and how frequently, are needs assessed?
   3.3 Describe any advisory bodies.

SERVICES:
1. What services are required to meet the objectives of the Learning Resources Program? Examples include:
   - Instructional Development
   - Audio Recording and Duplication
   - Faculty Development
   - Equipment Acquisition and Distribution
   - Materials Acquisition and Distribution
   - Electronic Maintenance
   - Instructional television services
   - Computer Assisted Instruction/Microcomputers
   - Supervised Student Production Facilities
   - Photography Services

SPECIAL SERVICES:
   1.1 Describe the objective each service is required to support.
   1.2 What evidence supports the requirement for each service?
2. How and to what extent is each service you list in the above section provided now?
   2.1 Does the Learning Resources Program maintain a centralized service? If so, does it have a monopoly on campus? If not, what other services are there on campus, what is the extent of their jurisdiction, and to whom do they report? What is the rationale for this?
   2.2 What factors (a) encourage or (b) discourage the offering of these services? Who initiates requests for these services? Who determines which services are offered?
   2.3 Describe methods used to evaluate the quality of, and responses to, services.
   2.4 To whom are services refused, and under what circumstances?
   2.5 What changes have been made in the past five years?
   2.6 What changes in service offerings are necessary (a) now, and (b) in five years, to fulfill the objectives of the Learning Resources Program?
3. How do existing services compare to the standards?
   3.1 What are the strengths and weaknesses of the staff's ability to provide the services described above?
   3.2. How are the services coordinated?
   3.3 Describe the changes you recommend to improve level and utilization of staff.
   3.4. How well do the experience and training of the staff relate to the services they are expected to provide? Does each service unit supervisor meet AECT certification standards?
   3.5. Are staff members adequately recognized and compensated for the work they perform?
   3.6. Describe the process whereby staff members are evaluated.

PHYSICAL FACILITIES, EQUIPMENT, AND MATERIALS:
1. Evaluate the physical facilities available to serve the Learning Resources Program.
   1.1 Describe all specialized instructional media facilities. Indicate how each supports the institution's objectives.
   1.2 What are the Learning Resources Program's strengths and weaknesses in facilities?
2. Report all Learning Resources Program equipment available to support the institution's goals. Note locations and ages of the equipment.
   2.1 Describe the program for systematic replacement of equipment.
   2.2 Indicate holdings not controlled by the Learning Resources Program.
   2.3 What are the program's strengths and weaknesses in equipment holdings?
3. Report all media materials holdings, and indicate how these support the institution's objectives.
   3.1 Describe the program for systematic replacement of materials.
   3.2 Indicate the holdings not controlled by the Learning Resources Program.
   3.3 What are the program's strengths and weaknesses in materials holdings?
4. What information is kept concerning the utilization of instructional media facilities, Learning Resources Program equipment, materials, and services.
5. What is the percentage of service requests that are refused because of insufficient equipment or materials?
6. Describe routine methods used to evaluate quality of and response to materials and equipment.
7. What special efforts are being made to assure effective utilization of instructional media facilities, materials, and equipment?
8. Describe the Learning Resources Program's involvement in planning, purchasing, controlling, and maintaining materials, facilities, and equipment.

MANAGEMENT/LEARNING RESOURCES PROGRAM DIRECTOR EVALUATION

INTRODUCTION

When conducting a self-study of a manager or a management team, several evaluation techniques are useful. None are absolutely foolproof processes, and results always must be understood in some context. The purpose of a performance appraisal is not to assess guilt, but to improve performance. If any of the following methods are used to improve performance, positive results are more likely to occur.

THE CHECKLIST

This method of evaluation is quite simple and widely used. First, you list traits, and then you enter relative scores and comments as required. It is possible to elicit a lot of useful information is possible, but is done with some problems:

- Evaluators have different values for what is "normal", "above average", "excellent", and so on.
- A "Horns/Halo Effect" can dramatically affect the reviewer's scoring. If the evaluator feels a manager is terrible because of what he or she did at the office party last year, the "horns effect" masks a clear picture of the person's job-related performance. Likewise, if this same manager were reviewed by another evaluator who felt very positive about what he or she had done at the party, a "halo effect" would outshine the evaluation of job performance.

RESULTS-ORIENTED

A performance appraisal using this method should start before the period in which performance is to be evaluated. At that point, the manager and superior agree to what should happen in the time period to follow. At the end of the evaluation period, results are measured against written expectations. A Management by Objectives program (or "MBO" program) is a results-oriented performance appraisal.

Clear communication between boss and subordinate and identifiable standards or measures of performance are features of this method. However, there are some shortcomings:

- It is difficult to deviate from "means justify the end" when the goals are so explicit. The process of reaching goals should always be subordinate to the goals themselves; otherwise, people and other resources can be abused.

- The process of creating objectives can be very time-consuming in itself. Measurable, specific goals take time and skill to create.
- The goals that are included may not be the right ones for the organization. Although the goal may state that you should acquire a certain number of books in one year, your organization might be better served with fewer books and more films and videotapes.

CRITICAL INCIDENT

This method, while not easy to do at the end of an appraisal period, is excellent when applied throughout the period. By noting, in written form, observations of the manager's behavior during the time period, realistic feedback to the manager is possible. While the emphasis is on overt behavior, notations of what the manager did not do could improve future performance. You also can note a manager's stylistic preferences and whether or not they are helpful to the job.

The strength of this method is process appraisal, but there can be some shortcomings:

- It takes a lot of time to do this type of evaluation.
- The use of an impartial, outside, trained observer is recommended.
- Everyone may feel wonderful about the work situation and yet results are poor.

BEHAVIOR ANCHOR

This method is relatively new to appraising work performance. It is similar to the critical incident method, but is more structured. Within any given competency, specific hierarchical behaviors are described along a continuum. This allows a clear measurable evaluation of a person's performance as observed by others. It avoids many of the pitfalls of other methods, but it has some drawbacks of its own:

- It takes a great deal of time to construct meaningful competencies and behavioral anchors. Once these are described, however, evaluation is relatively fast and useful to both evaluator and the person being evaluated.
- In the case of personnel matters, results shall be reported in general terms.

MANAGEMENT/LEARNING RESOURCES PROGRAM DIRECTOR ESSAY EVALUATION INSTRUMENT

One of the easiest, most complete ways to appraise management performance is to simply have manager and evaluator write out their respective views about the strengths and weaknesses of the past time period and their expectations for the coming time period. These written essays can be exchanged before a meeting so that discussion is focused on the future and positive movement. The main problems are the limitations of the written and spoken word and the skill of both persons to use language to communicate.

MANAGEMENT ESSAY EVALUATION INSTRUMENT

Both evaluators and the manager being evaluated receive the same form. After each person has an opportunity to complete it, they exchange evaluations. The persons involved then meet to discuss and identify new goals, objectives and plan of action. The evaluator makes a written review of the meeting, but the evaluated person can also note important points for the record or can disagree with the outcome

The form that follows could be applied to any level of Learning Resources Program management and could be used as a simple form of review by outside peers or colleagues. Unless the peer group does some investigation of the manager's performance on its own, however, little if any meaningful progress can be expected.

ESSAY EVALUATION

Name of Evaluator(s) _____

Job Title _____

Name of Person Being Evaluated _____

Job Title _____

Reporting Period _____

Review Interview Date _____

Original Appointment Date _____

1. List accomplishments during the evaluation period and areas where person excels (the person's strengths).

2. In what areas does the person need to expand his or her knowledge of procedures, etc.? (The person's need for knowledge, attitudes or skills or areas for improvement).

3. What would it take for this person to be the best person at what he or she does?

4. State the three top priorities for this person for the coming year and briefly indicate how they will be accomplished.

5. Date of Meeting_____

    Review of Meeting (include issues raised, conclusions).

USER LEARNING RESOURCES PROGRAM EVALUATION TECHNIQUES

In addition to an intensive self-study of a Learning Resources Program, you should have mechanisms for continual evaluation of the Learning Resources Program. The following are recommended activities which will provide data for ongoing program evaluation.

1. **Continuous User Surveys.** Develop a short, succinct user evaluation form for each service area and distribute it to a representative sampling of service users at least monthly.

2. **Peer Reviews.** It can be very effective to have people from neighboring institutions perform an annual or semiannual peer review of the Learning Resources Program. This technique has the advantage of providing input from external professionals, but is not nearly as comprehensive as the assisted self-study and generally will consist of a one-day on-site visit.

3. **Collection of quantifiable standardized data.** AECT is considering undertaking a National Learning Resources Program Inventory. This would help establish a national database to which Learning Resources Programs could compare themselves. In order to participate in this national inventory, you should compile Learning Resources Program statistics locally on a regular basis. The standards call for some information to be reported in ways not traditionally used (for instance, the 5% turndown rate for equipment availability). The Learning Resources Program should study the Standards and the national inventory to determine appropriate program statistics to keep.

4. **Annual Report.** Develop an Annual Report on the Learning Resources Program that summarizes its status, budget, strengths, weaknesses, and goals for that year.

5. **Depreciation Schedules.** Equipment inventory depreciation should occur annually. In order to provide some basis for equipment life, this publication includes a table that summarizes average equipment life as determined by the 1986 survey conducted by the Inter-University Council of Media Directors at public universities in the state of Ohio. Adequate funds should be budgeted annually to replace equipment whose life span has ended. The standards recommend an average budget for equipment replacement of 12% of the value of the inventory. If the depreciation schedule indicates a higher amount of money is needed, then you should use the higher figure.

USER LEARNING RESOURCES PROGRAM EVALUATION:

A user evaluation instrument should be developed and administered as part of the self-study. Conciseness is critical, since a questionnaire that takes more than a few minutes to complete is not likely to be taken seriously by recipients without follow-up reminders and encouragement. Items should be designed to facilitate data tabulation and analysis.

The first step in developing a questionnaire is identification of the specific information that is needed. If the amount of information is substantial, it may be appropriate to prepare several questionnaires, each focusing on different aspects of the Learning Resources Program's service, and then send them to different samples of the user population. As the individual questions are prepared, it is important to consider each very carefully. Does it provide the information desired? Will the information provided be of practical value to the Learning Resources Program? Items that appear to be trivial or provide data of little practical use should be deleted.

A sample survey form is found in Appendix A. Note the brevity of the form and the focus on specific aspects of the Learning Resources Program's service.

Following is a list of *potential* areas of concern for an evaluation instrument. It must be emphasized that under no circumstances should *all* of these items be incorporated into a single questionnaire. Evaluators should select only those items of specific interest to the Learning Resources Program. The following is in no way to be considered an all-inclusive list. Additional items should be developed according to the specific needs of the Learning Resources Program being evaluated.

1. Demographic information; including academic rank and departmental affiliation, rank or staff classification, length of time on campus.

2. Sources of patron information about Learning Resources Program Services and Facilities.

3. Where patrons obtain Learning Resources Program Services.

4. Faculty and staff use of specific services and facilities including frequency and satisfaction levels.

5. Student use, as assigned by faculty, of specific services and facilities including frequency and satisfaction levels.

6. Additional services, facilities and collections desired by patrons and their level of desire.

SUGGESTED USER LEARNING RESOURCES PROGRAM EVALUATION ITEMS

1. Demographic Information.
    - 1.1 Academic Staff. List academic departments, schools, and colleges with which the patron might be affiliated.
    - 1.2 Staff and Administration. List all offices, divisions, and research units which are not directly involved in instruction.
    - 1.3 Academic Rank. List all relevant academic ranks.
    - 1.4 Staff Classification. List all relevant classifications, or group in relevant functional groups (i.e. clerical).
    - 1.5 Time on Campus. Group time-spans for checkoff, such as two years or less, three to nine years, or ten years or more.

2. Sources of patron information about Learning Resources Program Services, collections, and facilities. List here all methods used to obtain information.
    - 2.1. Is adequate information available?
       ____Yes ___No

2.2 How were you informed about services and facilities? (List all means presently used)
    a. Handouts, Fact Sheets, Brochures
    b. New Faculty Orientation
    c. Personal visit to Learning Resources Program Services
    d. Faculty/Staff Telephone directory
    e. Colleague
    f. Other:_____

2.3 How can we get information to you? (List all possible means of communication)
    a. Department Meeting Presentations
    b. Written information sent directly to patron
    c. Faculty and Staff Orientations each Quarter/Semester
    d. Publish a Newsletter
    e. Articles in Campus Publications
    f. The Best Way to Get Information to me is: _____

3. Where Patrons Obtain Learning Resources Program Services and Facilities (List locations where the patron might be likely to obtain services if more than a single source of services exists).

4. Patron Use of Specific Services, Collections, and Facilities. (Include Frequency, Satisfaction, and Reasons if Service not used). This section of the Instrument will be the longest. Care should be taken to include all specific services offered, especially services mentioned in the standards. The following sample list of Services is intended to be a list from which to begin. It should be adapted to individual institutions, deleting or adding items as needed.

4.1 Development Services
    a. Faculty Development
        1. Seminars of Instructional Improvement
        2. Seminars or Teaching and Learning Research
        3. Seminars for Graduate "teaching" assistants
        4. Seminars on the Design of Instruction
        5. Other opportunities for Faculty self-improvement
    b. Instructional Development
        1. Assistance in Development of Instructional Materials
        2. Assistance in the Evaluation of Instructional Strategies
        3. Assistance in the Design and Development of Instructional Sequences
        4. Assistance in the Design and Development of Instructional Media

4.2 Creative/Production Services
    a. Graphic Services
        1. Preparation of Charts and Graphs
        2. Preparation of Art Work
    b. Photographic Services
        1. Photographic Processing
        2. Slide Duplication
        3. Illustrative Photography
        4. Location Photography
        5. Slide/Tape Program Development
        6. Portrait/Passport Photography
    c. Television Services
        1. Studio Production
        2. Location Production
        3. Post-Production Editing and Duplication
    d. Audio Services
        1. Production of Audio Recordings
        2. Narration of Audio Material
        3. Duplication of Audiotapes

4.3 Distribution Services
    a. Equipment
        1. Delivery of AV Equipment to classrooms
        2. Pick-up Service for AV Equipment
        3. Use of Classroom Installed Equipment
        4. Reservation of AV Equipment
    b. Materials
        1. Use of Media Collection
        2. Adequacy of Media Collection
        3. Use of Preview Facilities
        4. Use of Group Viewing Facilities
        5. Assistance in Rental/Borrowing of Off-Campus Materials

4.4 Maintenance and Engineering Services
    a. Media Equipment Repair and Maintenance
    b. Pick-up of Media Equipment for Repair
    c. On-Site repair of Media Equipment
    d. Consultation on Selection, Specifications, and Purchase of Media Equipment.
    e. Design of Instructional Technology Installations

4.5 Student Use of Facilities and Services as assigned by Faculty (List all services, collections and facilities which might be assigned by faculty).
    a. Use of Reserved Media and Playback Materials for Classroom Assignments
    b. Use of Portable Production Equipment for Course Assignments
    c. Use of Studio Facilities for Course Assignments
    d. Use of a Self-Instruction Graphics Lab
    e. Staff Instruction in Equipment use, Graphics use, or Media Materials Use.
    f. Additional Services, Facilities, Materials Desired by Patrons. Include Level of Desire. List possible additions to services, even those which may not be financially feasible at present.

SAMPLE USER LEARNING RESOURCES PROGRAM QUESTIONNAIRE

The questionnaire in Appendix A is provided as an example of one that might be used at your institution. It cannot be overemphasized that questionnaire items must be identified and developed to survey the specific evaluation needs of the Learning Resources Program being evaluated.

TOWARDS A MODEL LRP

The question most often asked by media directors, aside from those asking for additional funding, is: "How do I measure up against other institutions?" In order to be more objective, future editions will include a matrix. The approach we will be taking will first ask that you locate your institution within the context of an institutional classification system based on size and scope of your institution. That will enable you to place your institution within a size and scope framework. Once you have done that you'll find the appropriate matrix which most closely matches the size and scope of your institution.

The highest rankings will result from your program's having the highest number of categories which fall into the "advanced" level. Because your institution does not fall into the overall advanced rating should not be construed to mean that your program is inferior; what it should tell you is that there are specific areas indicated wherein possible improvements may be made. It is, in short, a self-evident mandate to you from AECT which, if shared with your administration, may open doors for change and hopefully, excellence.

The final step in the process of measurement of excellence will be that of ranking you in comparison with other institutions of similar size and scope. The Standards Committee is developing a mechanism cooperatively with AECT for collecting national statistics on LRPs through a national databank. Once established and when the databank has a sufficient number of entries, a subsequent ranking can then be made. This information should prove most valuable to you as you continue to seek programmatic improvement within your institution.

One final word: the results of the national rankings will receive national attention as their annual publication occurs. As with other national organizations, such information often forms the basis of change, hopefully for the better, on the part of the institutions ranked. Initially, we expect that institutions will submit data on a voluntary basis, so that a base databank can be assembled. As time goes on, however, the linkage between your program and the Standards will become much closer, given the prospect that various of the accrediting agencies will be adopting the Standards as a source of evaluative criteria. Once this happens, the option of volunteering information will most likely be replaced by that of having the data included as a integral part of the accreditation process. In either case, the ultimate aim remains the same: the improvement of instruction.

APPENDIX A:

Sample User

Learning Resources Program

Questionnaire

APPENDIX A

Media Center

FACULTY SURVEY

DIRECTIONS: The Media Center wishes to obtain information regarding faculty perceptions of its current and proposed services. Please respond to the questions below and return the survey form to us in the enclosed envelope by _____ if at all possible. The questionnaire should take about five minutes to complete. Your input is very important to us in our efforts to improve services to our faculty clients. Thank you. (The numbers in circles are for data compilation purposes only. Please disregard them.)

PART I. RESPONDENT PROFILE

1. Please check the College in which you hold your faculty appointment. If you hold a joint appointment, check all that apply.

    ①
    ___ Agriculture   ___ Business   ___ Design
    ___ Education   ___ Engineering   ___ Family/Consumer Science
    ___ Sciences and Humanities ___ Veterinary Medicine

2. Please check you faculty rank.

    ②
    ___ Professor   ___ Associate Professor   ___ Assistant Professor
    ___ Instructor   ___ Adjunct (rank)   ___ Teaching Assistant

3. How long have you been a faculty member?

    ③
    ___ 2 years or less   ___ 3 to 5 years   ___ 6 to 9 years
    ___ 10 years or more

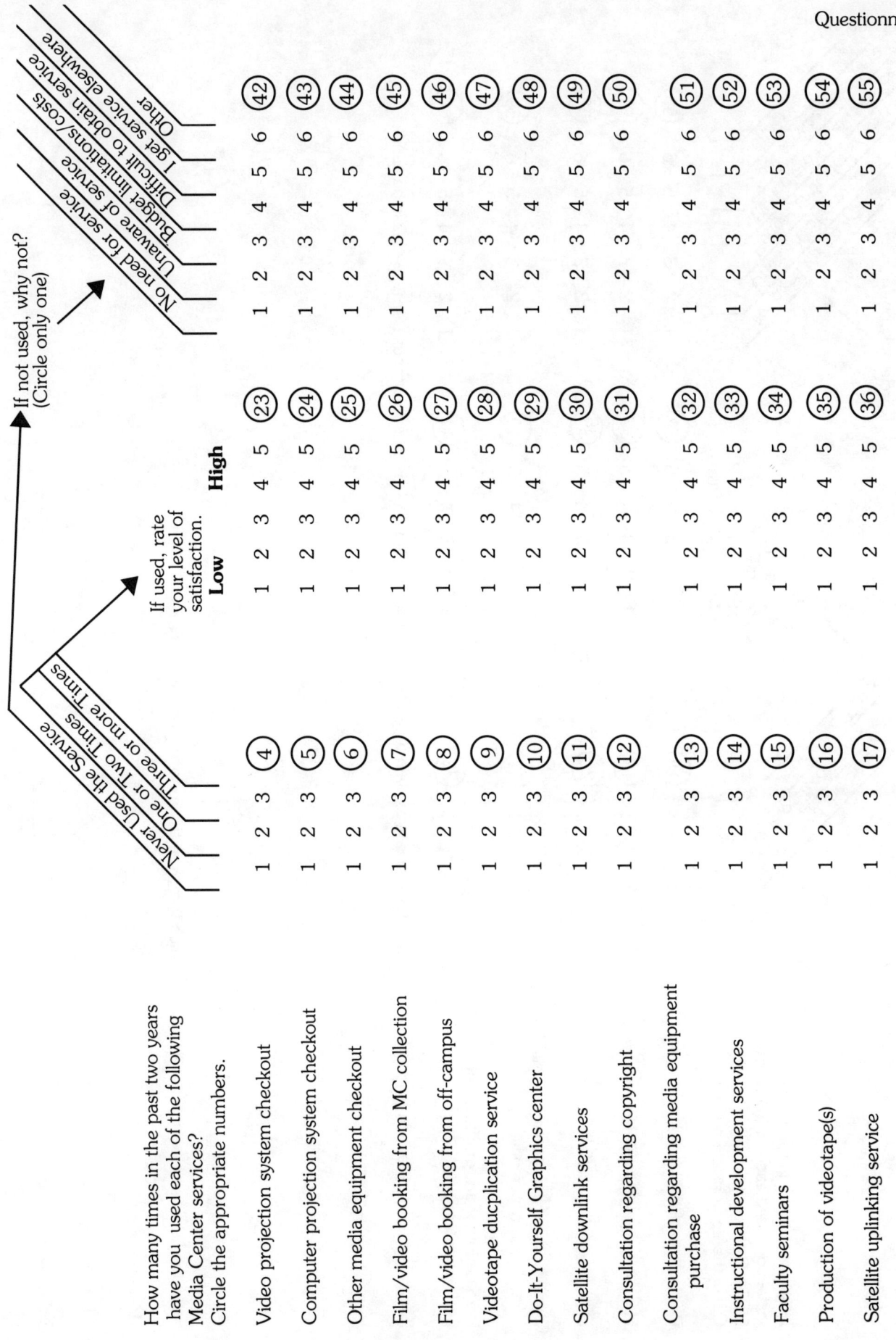

PART II. PRESENT MEDIA CENTER SERVICES

1. How many times in the past two years have you used each of the following Media Center services? Circle the appropriate numbers.

   Column headings (left group): Never Used the Service | One or Two Times | Three or more Times

   If used, rate your level of satisfaction. Low — High

   If not used, why not? (Circle only one): No need for service | Unaware of service | Budget limitations/costs | Difficult to obtain service | I get service elsewhere | Other

Service	Usage	Satisfaction	Reason not used
Video projection system checkout	1 2 3 (4)	1 2 3 4 5 (23)	1 2 3 4 5 6 (42)
Computer projection system checkout	1 2 3 (5)	1 2 3 4 5 (24)	1 2 3 4 5 6 (43)
Other media equipment checkout	1 2 3 (6)	1 2 3 4 5 (25)	1 2 3 4 5 6 (44)
Film/video booking from MC collection	1 2 3 (7)	1 2 3 4 5 (26)	1 2 3 4 5 6 (45)
Film/video booking from off-campus	1 2 3 (8)	1 2 3 4 5 (27)	1 2 3 4 5 6 (46)
Videotape ducplication service	1 2 3 (9)	1 2 3 4 5 (28)	1 2 3 4 5 6 (47)
Do-It-Yourself Graphics center	1 2 3 (10)	1 2 3 4 5 (29)	1 2 3 4 5 6 (48)
Satellite downlink services	1 2 3 (11)	1 2 3 4 5 (30)	1 2 3 4 5 6 (49)
Consultation regarding copyright	1 2 3 (12)	1 2 3 4 5 (31)	1 2 3 4 5 6 (50)
Consultation regarding media equipment purchase	1 2 3 (13)	1 2 3 4 5 (32)	1 2 3 4 5 6 (51)
Instructional development services	1 2 3 (14)	1 2 3 4 5 (33)	1 2 3 4 5 6 (52)
Faculty seminars	1 2 3 (15)	1 2 3 4 5 (34)	1 2 3 4 5 6 (53)
Production of videotape(s)	1 2 3 (16)	1 2 3 4 5 (35)	1 2 3 4 5 6 (54)
Satellite uplinking service	1 2 3 (17)	1 2 3 4 5 (36)	1 2 3 4 5 6 (55)

Questionnaire 41

PART II. PRESENT MEDIA CENTER SERVICES (Continued)

1. How many times in the past two years have you used each of the following Media Center services?
   Circle the appropriate numbers

   Columns: Never Used the Service | One or Two Times | Three or more Times

   If used, rate your level of satisfaction. **Low** — **High**

   If not used, why not? (Circle only one): No need for service | Unaware of service | Budget limitations/costs | Difficult to obtain service | I get service elsewhere | Other

Service	Usage	Satisfaction	Reason not used
Production of slide/tape	1 2 3 (18)	1 2 3 4 5 (37)	1 2 3 4 5 6 (56)
Photography service (taking pictures)	1 2 3 (19)	1 2 3 4 5 (38)	1 2 3 4 5 6 (57)
Film processing services	1 2 3 (20)	1 2 3 4 5 (39)	1 2 3 4 5 6 (58)
Preparation of computer-generated slides/transparencies	1 2 3 (21)	1 2 3 4 5 (40)	1 2 3 4 5 6 (59)
Preparation of art, graphics, etc., for publication(s)	1 2 3 (22)	1 2 3 4 5 (41)	1 2 3 4 5 6 (60)

2. If your level of satisfaction is low (1 or 2) on any item, please explain why you were not satisfied. This is an anonymous form, so please be candid.

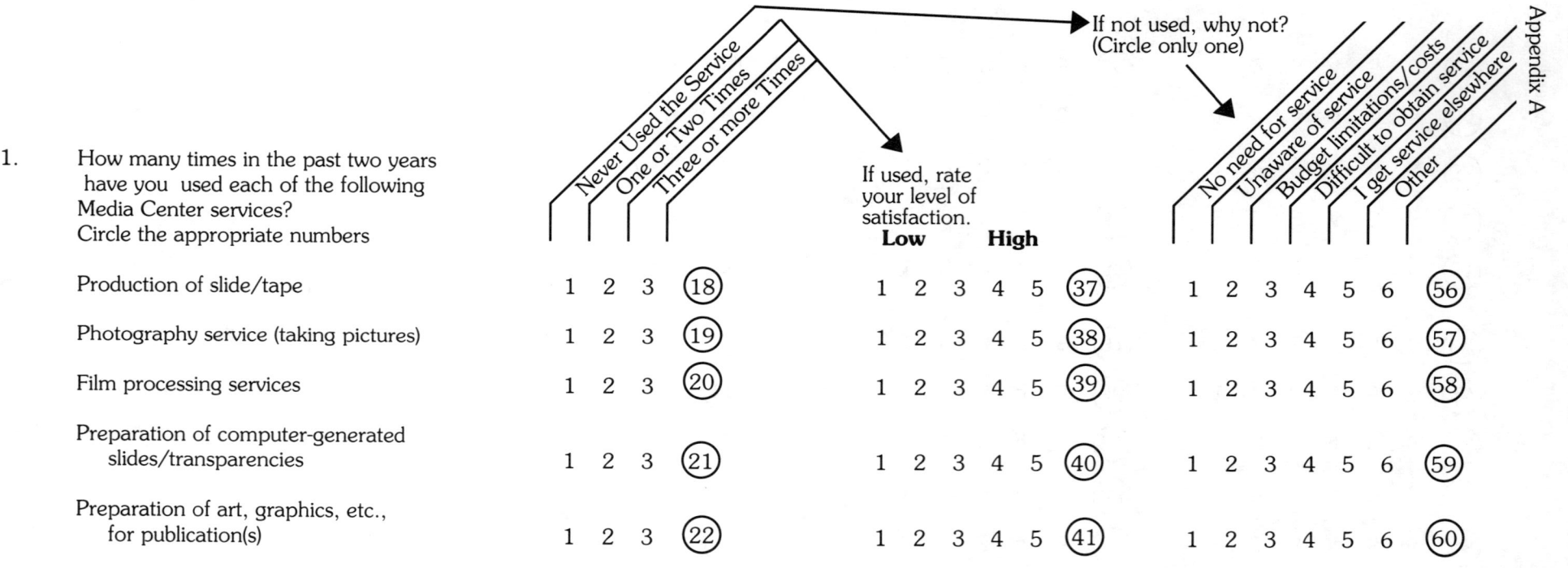

3. From the list of services in item #1 above, which three are the most important to you?

   Most important   # _____

   (61) 2nd most important   # _____

   3rd most important   # _____

Appendix A

PART III. PROPOSED MEDIA CENTER SERVICES

1. The Media Center is looking for ways in which it can expand its services to the faculty. Which of the following would be of interest to you?

	Yes	No	No Opinion
Short-term microcomputer check-out			○ 62
Assistance in developing/adapting instructional software for microcomputers			○ 63
Assistance in developing instructional software for VAX (LAN, etc.) system			○ 64
MacIntosh microcomputer in Do-It-Yourself Graphics			○ 65
VHS video edit system in Do-It-Yourself Graphics			○ 66
Printing/binding facilities in Do-It-Yourself Graphics			○ 67
Activate campus cable system to permit deliver of lectures to multiple classrooms			○ 68
Activate campus cable system to enhance intro-campus communications (e.g., bulletin board, professional development programming, presentations by administrators and campus groups, videoconferencing)			○ 69
Expand instructional development (course-related) activities			○ 70
Expand services in faculty/professional development areas			○ 71
Publish periodic newsletter on topics related to teaching and learning at our institutuion			○ 72
Expand desktop publishing capability			○ 73
Provide additional equipment support for evening classes			○ 74
Expand video/computer projection capability in large classrooms			○ 75

2. From the list above, which three items would be most important to you?

○ 76 Most important # _____ 2nd most important # _____ 3rd most important # _____

IV. COMMENTS

1. (Optional) Do you have comments or recommendations for the Media Center? Please attach an additional sheet if more space is needed.

Questionnaire   43

Appendix A

LEARNING RESOURCES–FACULTY/STAFF SURVEY (1)-(4) (5) 1

Please answer all questions in reference to the *Learning Resources* Services Department unless another facility is specifically mentioned. Ignore all circled numbers; these will be used for data tabulation. Thank you for taking time to answer all questions.

(6)-(8) Academic Department _____ name _____   OR   Admnistrative Office _____ name _____

(9)-(10) Academic Schools and Colleges _____   OR   _____ Adminstration _____

1. ____ Architecture
2. ____ Business Administration
3. ____ Education
4. ____ Engineering
5. ____ Hotel and Restaurant Management
6. ____ Humanities and Fine arts
7. ____ Law Center
8. ____ Natural Sciences and Math

9. ____ Optometry
10. ____ Pharmacy
11. ____ Social Sciences
12. ____ Social Work
13. ____ Technology
14. ____ Library
15. ____ Continuing Education

16. ____ Chancellor's Office
17. ____ Provost's Office
18. ____ Administrative Services Division
19. ____ Financial Affairs Division
20. ____ Student Life Division
21. ____ UH System
22. ____ Other (specify) _____

(11)-(12) Academic Rank _____   OR   _____ Staff Classification _____

1. ____ Professor
2. ____ Associate Professor
3. ____ Assistant Professor
4. ____ Instructor
5. ____ Teaching Assistant

9. ____ Lecturer
10. ____ Visiting Teacher
11. ____ Adjunct or Special Faculty
12. ____ Other (specify) _____

16. ____ Professional/Administrative'
17. ____ Technical/Service Craft
18. ____ Office/Clerical
19. ____ Other (specify) _____

(13) Length of Time at College/University

1. ____ 2 years or less
2. ____ 3 to 7 years
3. ____ 8 or more years

This survey takes approximately 15 minutes to complete. Please return in the attached envelope to

Questionnaire 45

I. In the following section, please respond in terms of where you get your audiovisual type of service. Listed below are some broad and some specific categories. Please circle the number(s) that best indicate where you obtain the service. More than one source may be circled if you use multiple sources to obtain a service.

A. WHERE DO YOU GET THE FOLLOWING CATEGORIES OF SERVICES?

Column headings (diagonal):
1. I do not use this service
2. AV Services Dept.
3. My college or department
4. Another on-campus source
5. An off-campus source
6. My personal resources/equipment

	Service	1	2	3	4	5	6	(item #s)
1.	AV Equipment for classroom or instructional purposes	1	2	3	4	5	6	15–20
2.	AV Equipment for other purposes (research, off-campus, personal, etc.)	1	2	3	4	5	6	21–26
3.	Photographic services (except slide processing)	1	2	3	4	5	6	27–32
4.	Slide film processing	1	2	3	4	5	6	33–38
5.	Preparation of art, graphs, and charts	1	2	3	4	5	6	39–44
6.	Production of video tapes	1	2	3	4	5	6	45–50
7.	Production of audio tapes	1	2	3	4	5	6	51–56
8.	AV Equipment repair and maintenance	1	2	3	4	5	6	57–62
9.	Assistance on AV equipment specifications and purchasing	1	2	3	4	5	6	63–68
10.	AV Supplies (lamps, audio and video tape, acetate rolls, etc.)	1	2	3	4	5	6	69–74
11.	Film and video tape rental/borrowing assistance	1	2	3	4	5	6	7–12
12.	Assistance in the planning and design of AV presentations	1	2	3	4	5	6	13–18
13.	Instructions on equipment operation and utilization	1	2	3	4	5	6	19–24

B. From the list of services above, which three are the most important to you?

25–26 Most Important # _____
27–28 2nd Most Important # _____
29–30 3rd Most Important # _____

46   Appendix A

II. In this section please respond in terms of how you have been informed about the various services offered by the central Audiovisual Services Department.

㉜

A. Do you feel you are adequately informed about the services Audiovisual Services provides?

1. _____ Yes   2. _____ No

B. How have you been informed? (Check all that apply)

㉝ _____ AV Handouts, Fact Sheet, Brochure
㉞ _____ New Faculty Orientation
㉟ _____ Visited *Learning Resources*
㊱ _____ Faculty and Staff Telelphone Directory
㊲ _____ Library Handbook for Faculty
㊳ _____ Faculty/Staff Handbook
㊴ _____ Library Media Services Handbook
㊵ _____ Colleague
㊶ _____ Other

C. What do you suggest we do to get information to you? (Check all that apply)

㊷ _____ Make presentations at departmental meetings
㊸ _____ Send information addressed to me (don't send copies to the department for distribution)
㊹ _____ Hold faculty and staff orientations each semester
㊺ _____ Publish a newsletter
㊻ _____ Articles in campus publications (student newspaper, etc.)
㊻ _____ The best way to get information to me is: _____

Questionnaire   47

III. In the following section, please respond in terms of your use or non-use of the following basic services performed by the various sections of the *Learning Resources Services Department*.

A. How many times in the past two years have you used each of the following services from Audiovisual Services? Circle the appropriate numbers.

Column headings (Frequency): Never Used the Service / One or Two Times / Three or more Times

If used, rate your level of satisfaction. (Low — High)

If not used, why not? (Circle only one): No need for service / Unaware of service / Budget limitations/costs / Difficult to obtain service / I get service elsewhere / Other

#	Service	Frequency	Satisfaction	Why Never Used?
1.	Preparation of charts and graphs	1 2 ③(49)	1 2 3 4 5 ⑤(50)	1 2 3 4 5 6 ⑤(51)
2.	Preparation of other art work	1 2 3 ㉚(52)	1 2 3 4 5 ㉝(53)	1 2 3 4 5 6 ㉞(54)
3.	Slide film processing	1 2 3 ㉟(55)	1 2 3 4 5 ㊱(56)	1 2 3 4 5 6 ㊼(57)
4.	Passport photography	1 2 3 (58)	1 2 3 4 5 (59)	1 2 3 4 5 6 (60)
5.	Production of slides and prints	1 2 3 (61)	1 2 3 4 5 (62)	1 2 3 4 5 6 (63)
6.	Illustrative photography	1 2 3 (64)	1 2 3 4 5 (65)	1 2 3 4 5 6 (66)
7.	Portrait photography	1 2 3 (67)	1 2 3 4 5 (68)	1 2 3 4 5 6 (69) ①—④
8.	Production of video tapes	1 2 3 (70)	1 2 3 4 5 (71)	1 2 3 4 5 6 (72)
9.	Editing and duplication of video tape	1 2 3 (73)	1 2 3 4 5 (74)	1 2 3 4 5 6 (75) ⑤—③
10.	Production of audio tapes	1 2 3 (7)	1 2 3 4 5 (8)	1 2 3 4 5 6 (9)
11.	Duplication of audio tapes	1 2 3 (10)	1 2 3 4 5 (11)	1 2 3 4 5 6 (12)
12.	Narration of audio tapes	1 2 3 (13)	1 2 3 4 5 (14)	1 2 3 4 5 6 (15)
13.	Assistance in Script Writing	1 2 3 (16)	1 2 3 4 5 (17)	1 2 3 4 5 6 (18)
14.	Synchronizing slide-tape program	1 2 3 (19)	1 2 3 4 5 (20)	1 2 3 4 5 6 (21)
15.	Vista I or Vista II rooms	1 2 3 (22)	1 2 3 4 5 (23)	1 2 3 4 5 6 (24)
16.	AV Equipment delivered to classroom	1 2 3 (25)	1 2 3 4 5 (26)	1 2 3 4 5 6 (27)
17.	Counter service for AV Equipment	1 2 3 (28)	1 2 3 4 5 (29)	1 2 3 4 5 6 (30)
18.	Use of AV equipment in projection booth	1 2 3 (31)	1 2 3 4 5 (33)	1 2 3 4 5 6 (33)
19.	Semester Booking of AV Equipment	1 2 3 (34)	1 2 3 4 5 (35)	1 2 3 4 5 6 (36)

Appendix A

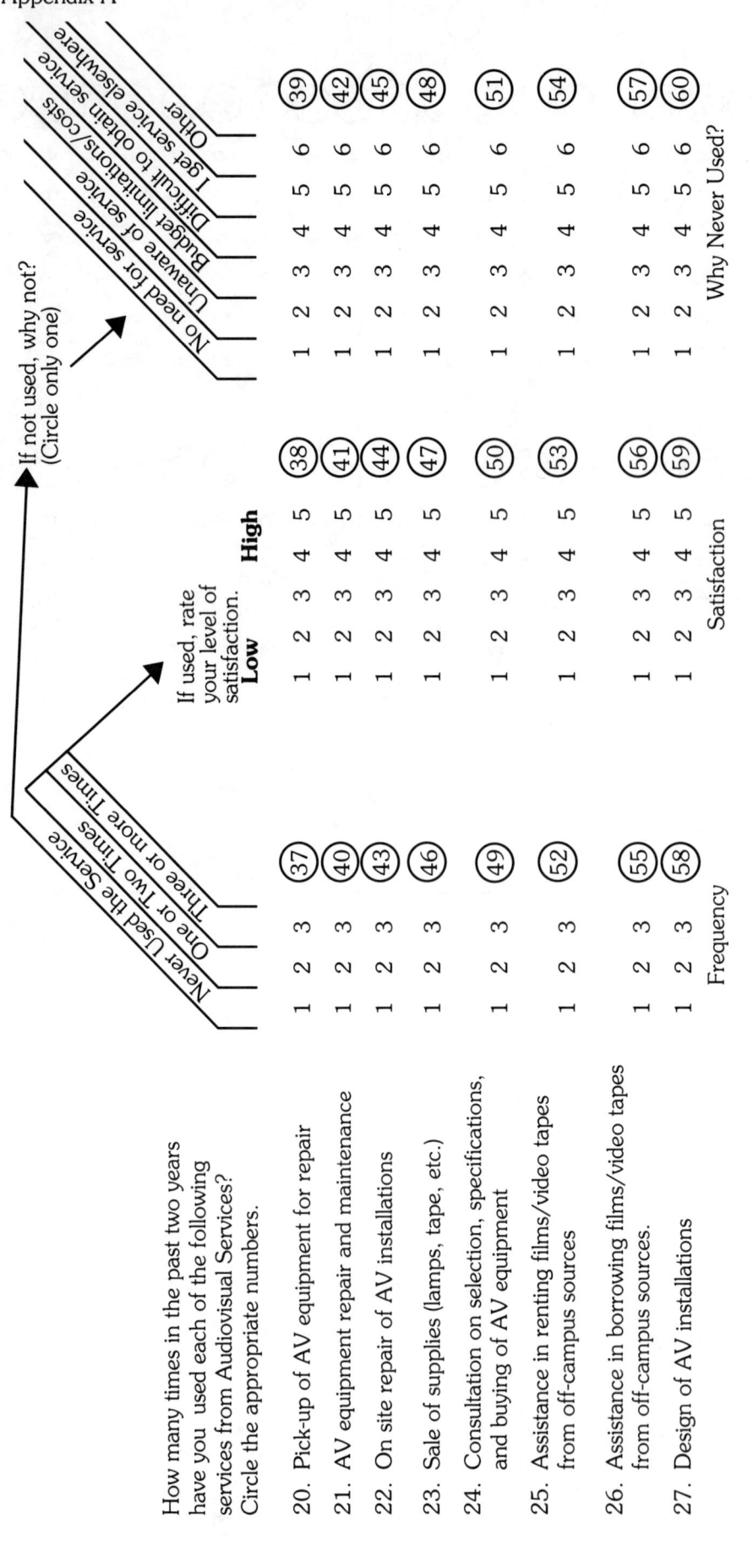

III. (Continued)

A. How many times in the past two years have you used each of the following services from Audiovisual Services? Circle the appropriate numbers.

Column headers (frequency): Never Used the Service / One or Two Times / Three or more Times

If used, rate your level of satisfaction. **Low** — **High**

If not used, why not? (Circle only one): No need for service / Unaware of service / Budget limitations/costs / Difficult to obtain service / I get service elsewhere / Other

Service	Frequency	Satisfaction	Why Never Used?
20. Pick-up of AV equipment for repair	1 2 3 (37)	1 2 3 4 5 (38)	1 2 3 4 5 6 (39)
21. AV equipment repair and maintenance	1 2 3 (40)	1 2 3 4 5 (41)	1 2 3 4 5 6 (42)
22. On site repair of AV installations	1 2 3 (43)	1 2 3 4 5 (44)	1 2 3 4 5 6 (45)
23. Sale of supplies (lamps, tape, etc.)	1 2 3 (46)	1 2 3 4 5 (47)	1 2 3 4 5 6 (48)
24. Consultation on selection, specifications, and buying of AV equipment	1 2 3 (49)	1 2 3 4 5 (50)	1 2 3 4 5 6 (51)
25. Assistance in renting films/video tapes from off-campus sources	1 2 3 (52)	1 2 3 4 5 (53)	1 2 3 4 5 6 (54)
26. Assistance in borrowing films/video tapes from off-campus sources.	1 2 3 (55)	1 2 3 4 5 (56)	1 2 3 4 5 6 (57)
27. Design of AV installations	1 2 3 (58)	1 2 3 4 5 (59)	1 2 3 4 5 6 (60)

B. If your level of satisfaction is low an any item, please specify the cause of your dissatisfaction.

Questionnaire 49

⑤ ___ ④ ___

①-④ ___

IV. This section pertains to 16mm motion picture films/videotape collections housed in and distributed by the central Audiovisual Services Department.

⑦ A. Have you used a motion picture film/video in the last two years?

1. ___ Yes
2. ___ No (Go to questions D and E)

B. If <u>yes</u>, where do you get the films/video you see? (Check all that apply)

⑧ ___ Film/video collection in Audiovisual Services
⑨ ___ Department or college
⑩ ___ Rent films/video from off-campus
⑪ ___ Borrow free films/video from off-campus
⑫ ___ Other (specify) _____

C. If you have used the film/video collection in *Learning Resources*, please circle your level of satisfaction with this collection.

   Low   **High**

⑬   1   2   3   4   5

D. What would encourage you to use motion picture films/video? (Check all that apply)

⑭ ___ The establishment of a large up-to-date film and video collection that has a budget to buy more titles
⑮ ___ Somone, other than requesting department, to pay the cost of renting films and videotapes.
⑯ ___ Provide library reference service for the research and selection of appropriate films and videotapes to buy or rent
⑰ ___ Expand the film and videotape collection
⑱ ___ Other (specify) _____

E. Knowing that resources are limited, please indicate the importance <u>you</u> place upon a large centralized, up-to-date motion picture film and videotape collection. (Check only one)

1. ___ Essential
2. ___ Desirable
3. ___ Unimportant
4. ___ No opinion

⑲

50   Appendix A

V. | This section pertains to the Library Media Center located in your library. This facility is operated by the Library, not by the *Learning Resources Services Department*. |

(20) A. Do you use or assign students to use audiovisual materials (audio and video tapes, filmstrips, slides, films, multi-media, etc.) in a resources center of some kind?

   1. _____ Yes
   2. _____ No (Go to questions D and E)

B. If yes, where do you do this? (Check all that apply)

   (21) _____ Library Media Center in the Library
   (22) _____ My college's Media Center/Learning Resources Center/Specialized Lab
   (23) _____ My department's facility
   (24) _____ Other (specify) _____

C. If you have used or assigned students to use the Library Media Center, please circle your level of satisfaction with this facility.

   Low　　　　　　　　　　**High**
   (25)　1　　2　　3　　4　　5

D. What would encourage you to use or assign students to use a centralized facility like the Library Media Center, where a collection of audiovisual materials would be available many hours a day, weekends, and holidays? (Check all that apply)

   (26) _____ A large up-to-date collection of audiovisual materials, with a budget to acquire more
   (27) _____ Professional staff members on duty to assist faculty and students
   (28) _____ A facility equipped for using *all* types of materials (16mm films, 1/2" videocassette tape, video disk, etc.)
   (29) _____ Other (specify) _____

(30) E. Knowing that resources are limited, please indicate the importance you place upon a centralized, Library Media Center. (Check only one)

   1. _____ Essential
   2. _____ Desirable
   3. _____ Unimportant
   4. _____ No opinion

VI. Knowing Audiovisual Services has limited resources which of these do you think we should seriously consider initiating or extending?

		Yes	No	No Opinion	
1.	Establish and reserve for frequent media users, specially equipped general purpose classrooms.	1	2	3	(31)
2.	Provide pick-up/delivery of films borrowed from local Community College.	1	2	3	(32)
3.	Provide additional equipment support for evening classes.	1	2	3	(33)
4.	Offer in-service and workshops to faculty and staff.	1	2	3	(34)
5.	Permanently assign AV equipment to all general purpose classrooms.	1	2	3	(35)
6.	Provide a video classroom/studio where a presentation can be easily and unobtrusively video taped.	1	2	3	(36)
7.	Establish a facility where faculty and staff can produce their own AV materials.	1	2	3	(37)
8.	Offer personal (non job related) services to the faculty and staff.	1	2	3	(38)
9.	Acquire video projectors for large screen projection in classrooms and auditoria.	1	2	3	(39)
10.	Assist faculty in revising instruction, utilizing media.	1	2	3	(40)
11.	Other (specify) _____	1	2	3	(41)

From the list above, which three items are most important to you?

(42)(43) Most Important #____
(44)(45) 2nd Most Important #____
(46)(47) 3rd Most Important #____

Do you have comments or recommendations for Audiovisual Services? (Attach a sheet if this is not enough space)

Questionnaire 51

APPENDIX B:

Equipment

Depreciation

Schedule

APPENDIX B

EQUIPMENT DEPRECIATION SCHEDULE

In assessing the real cost of equipment, it is important to consider the estimated years of life for a particular type of machine. Each unit of equipment will use a specific percentage of the unit's total cost per year. For example, a particular 16mm projector costs $800 and is expected to have a useful life of five years. Using the "straight-line" or "constant rate" method, the projector would "cost" $160 per year for five years.

When you use only annual budgets, it is easy to lose sight of costs that will occur outside of that budget. Furthermore, without recording these costs, it is difficult to assess the true value of the equipment available and the point where a unit of equipment should be removed from active service. Consequently, to keep a pool of equipment at a given level, new equipment must be purchased each year to match the combined annual depreciated cost of all equipment in service during the year.

DETERMINING THE USEFUL LIFE OF EQUIPMENT

No one schedule of expected years of use for a variety of equipment types will suffice for every institution, but each institution should be responsible for determining what is the useful life of its particular equipment. The following considerations should help determine that schedule:

1. For how many hours will a particular type of equipment be operated annually?
2. How often will a particular type of equipment be moved?
3) Will this type of equipment be used by a few people or many different people?
4) How fragile is a particular equipment type? Is it heavy duty? Is it designed for only occasional use?
5) Are faculty using a particular type of equipment more each year? less? about the same?
6) At what condition is a particular type of equipment unsatisfactory for use in the service? 10 percent of the time? 25 percent? 50 percent?

The amount of use is the most critical factor in determining the life expectancy for a given type of equipment. The more often a type of equipment is used annually, the fewer years it will be usable. Particular types of equipment may be designed for portability, but at some institutions they are fixed in specific locations, (e.g., overheads permanently fixed in a classroom, screens mounted above chalkboards). The more often an equipment type is moved, the fewer years it will be usable.

Furthermore, the kind of movement (through smooth corridors or over rough pavement) also is a factor. The more gentle the transfer, the greater the number of useful years a particular equipment type will be usable.

The people who will be operating this type of equipment, their number, their training and their experience will also affect the number of useful years expected from a particular equipment type. The greater the number of unskilled operators, the fewer the years of useful life that can be anticipated.

A particular type of equipment has its own system design characteristics as well. Some types of equipment are built like long distance commercial tractor-trailers, rugged, dependable, with a wide tolerance for acceptable operation. Others are delicate, sensitive electro-mechanical systems that have a critical tolerance for acceptable operation. Some systems are simple, others are extremely intricate and complex. The simpler and more rugged a particular system is the greater the number of useful years of service that can be expected.

The trends of use will affect the number of years too. If users are going to be using a particular type of equipment more in the future, the expected useful life of that equipment type will be less.

The more difficult thing to assess is when a particular type of equipment is no longer usable. Each institution will find someone who can point to an overhead projector purchased in 1952 and say, "What do you mean usable life, it still works doesn't it?" Yes, it may work when you go to use it, but what is the probability that it won't? What will customers tolerate when they schedule a unit of equipment for a class or seminar? Will they be willing to tolerate a 50-50 probability? or are they expecting something closer to perfect - 100%?

The guidelines are flexible and will allow either of these alternatives to be possible as well as any decision on the other consideration, but really any are valid as long as it reflects the situation at a particular institution.

INTER-UNIVERSITY COUNCIL OF MEDIA DIRECTORS

Audiovisual Equipment Longevity in Years—1986 data / 1976 data

Service	Equipment Type	Mean (1986)	Median (1986)	Mean (1976)	Median (1976)
Portable	16 mm Motion Pic Projector	8.6	8.0	7.5	7.5
Fixed		11.4	12.0		
Portable	Super 8mm Proj, Silent	5.3	5.0	4.8	4.5
Fixed		8.8	10.0		
Portable	Super 8mm Proj, Sound	5.6	5.0	5.1	5.0
Fixed		8.3	10.0		
Portable	Slide proj, Automatic	9.4	10.0	6.3	5.5
Fixed		11.6	12.0		
Portable	Slide proj, Manual	10.0	10.0	9.0	10.0
Fixed		12.2	14.0		
Portable	Discrete Slide-tape synchronizer	6.9	7.5	5.3	5.0
Fixed		9.6	10.0		
Portable	Combination slide & cassette unit	7.1	7.0		
Fixed		9.1	8.0		
Portable	Slide-Dissolve Unit	8.3	8.0	6.4	5.0
Fixed		10.2	10.0		
Portable	Filmstrip Projector Automatic	9.3	8.0		
Fixed		10.5	10.0		
Portable	Filmstrip Projector Manual	10.4	9.5	7.6	7.5
Fixed		11.2	10.5		
Portable	Combination Filmstrip & Cassette Unit	8.3	8.0		
Fixed		8.8	10.0		
Portable	Overhead Projector	10.0	10.0	7.6	8.0
Fixed		13.1	12.0		
Portable	Opaque Projector	12.4	12.0	8.0	8.0
Fixed		15.1	15.0		
Portable	Audio Tape Recorder Open Reel	8.4	8.0	6.5	6.5
Fixed		10.3	10.0		
Portable	Audio Cassette Recorder	6.5	7.0	5.0	4.5
Fixed		9.1	10.0		
Portable	Video Tape Recorder Open Reel	6.4	5.0	4.7	4.5
Fixed		7.5	6.5		
Portable	Video Cassette Recorder, VHS/Beta	6.3	6.0		
Fixed		7.6	7.5		
Portable	Video Cassette 3/4 U-matic	7.5	7.5	4.7	5.0
Fixed		8.8	8.0		
Portable	Video Camera	5.9	6.0	6.0	6.0
Fixed		7.9	8.0		
Portable	Video Monitor	7.9	8.0	7.0	8.0
Fixed		10.0	10.0		
Portable	Video Receiver	7.1	7.5	5.3	5.5
Fixed		9.3	10.0		
Portable	Video Projector	5.3	5.0		
Fixed		7.7	7.5		
Fixed	Proj. Screen, Wall	14.8	15.0	6.8	6.5
Portable	Proj. Screen, tripod	6.8	7.0	4.0	4.0
Fixed	Proj. Screen-auditorium	16.0	15.0	10.0	10.0
Portable	Projection cart	14.0	12.0	7.3	9.0
Fixed		14.2	13.5		
Portable	Portable sound system	6.1	6.0	5.6	5.0
Fixed		8.3	8.0		
Portable	Microphone	4.9	5.0	3.8	3.0
Fixed		6.9	7.0		
Portable	Record Player	8.9	8.5	6.3	5.5
Fixed		9.3	9.0		
Fixed	Desktop Computer	5.8	6.0		
Fixed	Floppy Disk Drive	5.6	6.0		
Portable	Computer Monitor	6.0	5.5		
Fixed		6.5	6.5		
Portable	Computer Printer	4.5	4.5		
Fixed		5.8	6.0		

Reference: Post, Richard. "Longevity and Depreciation of Audiovisual Equipment." *TechTrends.* Association for Educational Communications and Technology, Washington, DC. November, 1987, pp. 12-14.

Note: The Inter-University Council of Media Directors includes the directors of all campuswide audiovisual media service programs at public universities in the state of Ohio.

APPENDIX C:

References

APPENDIX C

REFERENCES

Albright, Michael J. "The Status of Media Centers in Higher Education." *Media Management Journal*, Spring 1984, pp.4-17. (Also ERIC Document Reproduction Service No. ED 242 306).

Albright, Michael J. "The Instructional Improvement Function: An Approaching Imperative in Higher Education." In Elwood E. Miller (Ed.), 1986 *Educational Media and Technology Yearbook*. Littleton, Colo.: Libraries Unlimited, 1986, pp. 71-82.

Association for Educational Communications and Technology. *College Learning Resources Programs: A Book of Readings*. Washington, DC: AECT, 1977.

Berling, John G. "The Technology of Learning Resources Services in Higher Education." In Elwood E. Miller (Ed.), 1985 *Educational Media and Technology Yearbook*. Littleton, Colo.: Libraries Unlimited, 1985. pp. 75-80.

Brong, Gerald R., Ed. *Media in Higher Education: The Critical Issues*. Pullman, Washington: Information Futures, Inc., 1976.

Calhoun, Judith G., et al. "A Computerized Approach to Management of Utilization Data in a Media Center." *Technical Horizons in Education*, 6:6, Nov 1979, pp.50-51.

Carnegie Council on Policy Studies in Higher Education. *A Classification of Institutions of Higher Education* (revised edition). Berkeley, California: Carnegie Council of Policy Studies in Higher Education, 1976.

Cornell, Richard A. "Whatever Became of Task Force Number 4?" Letter to AECT President Richard Gilkey, September, 1976.

Cornell, Richard A. "Emerging Technologies: Reaching Your Students; Bridging the Gap." *Ideas in Education*. Orlando, FL: University of Central Florida, College of Education, Fall, 1984.

Cornell, Richard A. *Perception and Utilization of an Instructional Resources Center by University Faculty Members: First Steps Toward Output Assessment*. Ft. Lauderdale, FL: Nova University, Doctoral Dissertation, August, 1981, p.168.

Crossman, David T. "The Library and Instructional Technology: An Open Marriage," in *Media in Higher Education: The Critical Issues*. Pullman, Washington: Information Futures, Inc., 1976.

Davis, John A. *Instructional Improvement - An Assessment of Programs at Sixteen Universities*. Pullman, Washington: Information Futures, Inc., 1976.

Davis, John, ed. *Guide for Self-Study of Media/ Educational Technology Service Programs in Higher Education: A Report to the Northwest Association of Schools and Colleges*. Prepared by the Northwest College and University Council for Management of Educational Technology, 1979.

Dennison, Linda T. "The Chargeback System: Useful Tool or Useless Hindrance?" *Media Management Journal*, Spring 1985, pp. 9-14.

Dillon, Connie. "Building from the Ground Down." *Media Management Journal*, Fall 1986, pp. 6-11.

Evans, Alan D. "The Manager Evaluates Educational Technology Services with Faculty Input." *Media Management Journal*, Fall 1984, pp. 12-15.

Gallup, David A. "Determining the Cost Effectiveness of Instructional Technology." *Educational Technology*, February 1977, p. 34.

Gray, Robert E. "Humanistic Media Management: Made in Japan." *Media Management Journal*, Fall 1984, pp. 10-12.

Gray, Robert E. "In Search of Excellence in Media Management: Lessons from America's Best-Run Companies." *Media Management Journal*, Spring 1985, pp. 3-5.

Gropper, George L. "On Gaining Acceptance for Instructional Design in a University Setting." *Educational Technology*, 17:12, p. 7, December, 1977.

Heath, Stanley P. and Donald C. Orlich, "Determining the Costs of Educational Technology: An Exploratory Review and Analysis." *Educational Technology*, 1972, p. 26, February ,1977.

Hinz, Marian, Robert Hinz, and Robert Jones. *Integrated Learning Resource Centers*. Pullman, WA,: Information Futures, Inc., 1980.

Hurst, Fred M. "Design Considerations for a Centralized Media Center." *Media Management Journal*, Fall 1986, pp.2-6.

International Council For Computers in Education."ICCE Policy Statement on Network and Multiple Machine Software." *The Computing Teacher*, pp.18-22,Sept. 1983.

Inventory of Policy and Program for Instructional Technology. Ad Hoc Committee on Instructional Technology, Commission on Research and Service, North Central Association of Colleges and Schools, Barton L. Griffith, Chairman. 1975.

Jones, Mary Ellen. "AV's Place in Small Liberal Arts Colleges." *Audiovisual Instruction*, 24:9, Dec. 1979, pp. 32-34.

Kanter, Rosabeth Moss. *Men and Women of the Corporation.* New York: Basic Books, Inc. 1977.

Kent, Alvin. "Money Management in a Media Resources Environment." *Media Management Journal*, Spring 1983, pp. 2-6.

Lawrason, Robin E. and Parkhurst, Bruce. "Media Resource Center Management in Higher Education: New Organizations for the Times." *NALLD Journal*, Winter 1985, pp. 9-27.

Lied, James R. "Lifetime Expectancy of Media Equipment." *Ohio Media Spectrum*, Fall 1979, Vol. 31, No. 3, pp. 64-67.

Lied, James R. "What's the Bottom Line for Your Media Center?." *Audiovisual Instruction*, February 1979, Vol. 24, No. 2, pp. 21-24, 61.

Lied, James R. "Beyond the Budget." *Instructional Innovator*, October 1980, Vol 25, No. 7, pp. 20-24.

Liesener, James W. *A Systematic Process for Planning Media Programs.* Chicago: American Library Association, 1976.

Marsh, Paul. *Development of a Media Services Management Model for Montana State University.* (Doctoral Dissertation, University of Washington, Seattle, 1979). Dissertation Abstracts International, 1980, 40, 623A.

Meierhenry, W. C. "Can the College and University Survive? Role of Media in the Future of Higher Education." *Media in Higher Education: The Critical Issues.* Pullman, WA, Information Futures, Inc., 1976.

Merrill, Irving, R., and Harold W. Drob. *Criteria for Planning the College and University Learning Resources Center*, Washington, DC, AECT, 1977.

Minnella, C. Vincent, et al. "Film Library Information Management System." Paper presented in Cortland, NY, June, 1979, Cortland, NY. (ERIC Document Reproduction Service, ED 179 194.)

Musahi, Miyamoto. *A Book of Five Rings - The Classic Guide to Strategy.*Woorstock, NY: The Overlook Press, 1982.

Office of the Chancellor, The California State University and Colleges. *Policy Statement on Instructional Development and Media Services.* Long Beach, California.: The California State University and 1977. Mimeo.

Pelletier, Pierre N. "Management of Educational Resources: An Alternative." *International Journal of Instructional Media*, Spring 1985, pp. 255-263.

Platte, James P. The Status and Prospects of Library/Learning Resources Centers at Michigan Community Colleges. Michigan Community College Community Services Association. 1979. (ERIC Document Reproduction Service No. ED 181 954).

Reicks, Donald. "The Need for Centralization." *Media in Higher Education: The Critical Issues.* Pullman, Washington: Information Futures, Inc., 1976.

Sakovitch, Vladimir. Guidelines for the Integration of College or University Library and Media Services. *Educational Technology*, 19:3, March 1979, p. 57-58.

Sayles, Leonard R. *Leadership - What Effective Managers Really Do... and How They Do It.* New York: McGraw-Hill Book Company, 1979.

Schmid, William T. *Media Center Management.* 1980. Hastings House Publishers, 10 East 40th Street, New York, New York 10016.

Schmidt, William D. *Learning Resources Programs That Make a Difference.* Washington, DC: Association for Educational Communications and Technology, 1986.

Spears, Robert E. "Are You Telling Your Story? Simple Strategies for Marketing Media Programs." *Media Management Journal*, Winter 1985, pp. 13-14.

Tiedemann, David A. "Use of the Delphi Technique to Plan Future Media Support Service Programs in Higher Education." *Media Management Journal*, Fall 1986, pp. 11-16.

U.S. Office of Education. *Educational Technology: A Handbook of Standard Terminology and a Guide for Recording and Reporting Information about Educational Technology. State Educational Records and Reports Series, Handbook X.* Washington, DC.: National Center for Educational Statistics, U. S. Office of Education, 1975.

VanUitert, D. Dean. "Adapting a Media Organization in a Changing Environment." *Media Management Journal*, Spring 1987, pp. 15-17.

Vlcek, Charles. "*Library Media Programs: Together We All Lose.*" Paper presented February 26, 1976, Richland, Washington.

Wilkening, Donald J. "A Production Lab the Faculty Can Call Their Own." *Audiovisual Instruction*, 24:9, Dec 1979, pp.24-25.

Wilson, Marlene. *Survival Skills for Managers*. Boulder, Colo.: Volunteer Management Associates, 1981.

APPENDIX D:

Contributors to the Standards

APPENDIX D

CONTRIBUTORS TO THE STANDARDS

Below is a list of Current and Former Members of The Association for Educational Communications and Technology: Postsecondary Guidelines Committee (formerly Postsecondary Guidelines: Task Force II for College and University Standards) and "Contributing Others" who gave valuable input to these standards.

TASK FORCE MEMBERS

Michael J. Albright
Iowa State University
Ames, Iowa

Alan Blair
Muskingum Technical College
New Concord, Ohio

Morell D. Boone
Eastern Michigan University
Ypsilanti, Michigan

Richard A. Cornell
University of Central Florida
Orlando, Florida

Kathleen B. Davey
Ohio State University
Columbus, Ohio

John A. Davis
Washington State University
Pullman, Washington

Alan D. Evans
Kent State University
Kent, Ohio

Lee Frischknecht
Arizona State University
Tempe, Arizona

Martin M. Goldberg
U.S. Merchant Marine Academy
Kings Point, New York

Jackie Hill
Paine College
Augusta, Georgia

Marian C, Hinz
Par-A-Docs
Jacksonville, Florida

Robert P. Hinz
Par-A-Docs
Jacksonville, Florida

Donald Huddleston
University of Hawaii at Manoa
Manoa, Hawaii

Robert T. Jones
Valdosta State College
Valdosta, Georgia

Dismas B. Kalcic
Benet Academy
Lisle, Illinois

Robert Kirchherr
Central Maine Voc. Tech. Inst.
Auburn, Maine

Shirley H. Lewis
University of Minnesota - Duluth
Duluth, Minnesota

James R. Lied
University of Cincinnati
Cincinnati, Ohio

Paul W. Marsh
Metropolitan Technical Community College
Omaha, Nebraska

Roland Mergener
Rhode Island College
Providence, Rhode Island

William B. Oglesby
University of Iowa
Iowa City, Iowa

James L. Page
Michigan State University
East Lansing, Michigan

Will D. Phillipson
University of Minnesota
Minneapolis, Minnesota

Robert E. Spears
Science App. Int. Corp.
Orlando, Florida

Stanton Rome
Quinsigamond Community College
Worcester, Massachusetts

Robert E. Stephens
Arkansas State University
State University, Arkansas

Joseph Schroeder
University of Houston
Houston, Texas

D. Dean VanUitert
Brigham Young University
Provo, Utah

David B. Walch
California Polytechnic State
University
San Luis Obispo, California

Hans Eric Wennberg
Elizabethtown College
Elizabethtown, Pennsylvania

"OTHER CONTRIBUTORS"

Richard Decker
Cuyahoga Community College
Cleveland, Ohio

John Hedberg
Western Australian Institute of
Technology,
Perth, Australia

Mrs. Donald Huddleston
Manoa, Hawaii

Mrs. Jan Jones
Valdosta, Georgia

Grame Murphy
University of Melbourne
Melbourne, Victoria, Australia

Dave Tiedemann
University of San Diego
Alcala Park, San Diego, California

Tim Spannaus
Southfield, Michigan

Al Mizell
Nova University
Ft. Lauderdale, Florida

George McNeal

Donald Johnson

John Childs